AMERICA FOREVER NEW

A Book of Poems

AMERICA
FOREVER
NEW

A Book of Poems

Compiled by
SARA and JOHN E. BREWTON

Drawings by Ann Grifalconi

Thomas Y. Crowell Company, New York

COMPILED BY
SARA AND JOHN E. BREWTON

Laughable Limericks
America Forever New: A Book of Poems

Contents

America is promises. We Americans
        . . . *have tomorrow*
        Bright before us
        Like a flame.

                                    —LANGSTON HUGHES

. . . *this New World is forever new to hands*
    that keep it new.

                                    —ARCHIBALD MAC LEISH

This Is Our Land

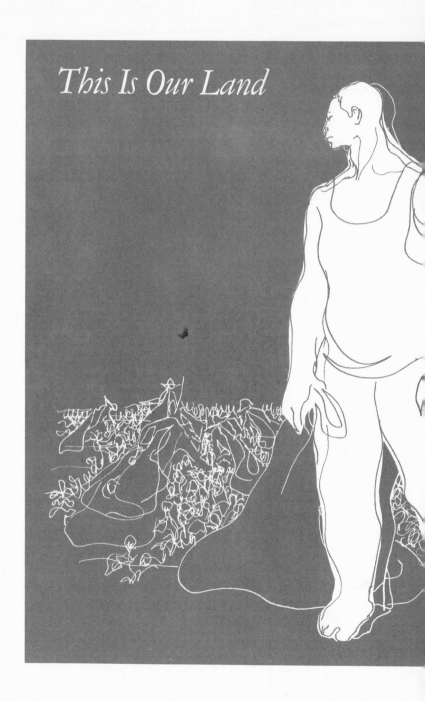

This, this is our land, this is our people,
This that is neither a land nor a race. We must reap
The wind here in the grass for our soul's harvest:
Here we must eat our salt or our bones starve.
Here we must live or live only as shadows.
This is our race, we that have none, that have had
Neither the old walls nor the voices around us,
This is our land, this is our ancient ground—
The raw earth, the mixed bloods and the strangers,
The different eyes, the wind, and the heart's change.
These we will not leave though the old call us.
This our country-earth, our blood, our kind.
Here we will live our years till the earth blind us—

ARCHIBALD MAC LEISH

OUR HERITAGE

We are a part of this rough land
Deep-rooted like the tree.
We've plowed this dirt with calloused hand
More than a century.

We know each cowbell's ringing here
Which tells the time of day.
We know the slopes to plant each year,
What our folks do and say.

We know the signals of each horn
And the messages they send
At set of sun or early morn
Upon a blowing wind.

When we lie down in bed at night
And hear a foxhorn blow,
We often rise, take lantern light,
Untie our hounds and go.

We like to follow hounds that chase
The fox until the morn
Then go back home with sleepy face
And on to plow the corn.

There is not one who does not love
A field and farming ground,
With sky and stars a roof above
And a companion hound!

We love this land we've always known
That holds us and our dead—
The rugged slopes with scattered stone
That grow our daily bread.

We love the lyric barking hound
And a piping horn that trills.
We love our high upheavaled ground,
Our heritage of hills.

JESSE STUART

AMERICAN NAMES

I have fallen in love with American names,
The sharp names that never get fat,
The snakeskin-titles of mining-claims,
The plumed war-bonnet of Medicine Hat,
Tucson and Deadwood and Lost Mule Flat.

Seine and Piave are silver spoons,
But the spoonbowl-metal is thin and worn,
There are English counties like hunting-tunes
Played on the keys of a postboy's horn,
But I will remember where I was born.

I will remember Carquinez Straits,
Little French Lick and Lundy's Lane,
The Yankee ships and the Yankee dates
And the bullet-towns of Calamity Jane.
I will remember Skunktown Plain.

* * * * *

Rue des Martyrs and Bleeding-Heart-Yard,
Senlis, Pisa, and Blindman's Oast,
It is a magic ghost you guard
But I am sick for a newer ghost,
Harrisburg, Spartanburg, Painted Post.

* * * * *

I shall not rest quiet in Montparnasse.
I shall not lie easy at Winchelsea.
You may bury my body in Sussex grass,
You may bury my tongue at Champmédy.
I shall not be there. I shall rise and pass.
Bury my heart at Wounded Knee.

STEPHEN VINCENT BENÉT

*L*OCALITIES

"Wagon Wheel Gap is a place I never saw
And Red Horse Gulch and the chutes of Cripple Creek.

"Red-shirted miners picking in the sluices,
Gamblers with red neckties in the night streets,
The fly-by-night towns of Bull Frog and Skiddoo.
The night-cool limestone white of Death Valley,
The straight drop of eight hundred feet
From a shelf road in the Hasiampa Valley:
Men and places they are I never saw.

"I have seen three White Horse taverns,
One in Illinois, one in Pennsylvania,
One in a timber-hid road of Wisconsin.

"I bought cheese and crackers
Between sun showers in a place called White Pigeon
Nestling with a blacksmith shop, a post-office,
And a berry-crate factory, where four roads cross.

"On the Pecatonica River near Freeport
I have seen boys run barefoot in the leaves
Throwing clubs at the walnut trees
In the yellow-and-gold of autumn,
And there was a brown mash dry on the inside of their
        hands.

"On the Cedar Fork Creek of Knox County
I know how the fingers of late October
Loosen the hazel nuts."

CARL SANDBURG

INDIAN NAMES

Ye say they all have passed away,
    That noble race and brave,
That their light canoes have vanished
    From off the crested wave;
That, 'mid the forests where they roamed,
    There rings no hunter's shout;
But their name is on your waters,
    Ye may not wash it out.

'Tis where Ontario's billow
    Like ocean's surge is curled;
Where strong Niagara's thunders wake
    The echo of the world;
Where red Missouri bringeth
    Rich tribute from the West,
And Rappahannock sweetly sleeps
    On green Virginia's breast.

Ye say their conelike cabins,
    That clustered o'er the vale,
Have fled away like withered leaves
    Before the autumn's gale:
But their memory liveth on your hills,
    Their baptism on your shore;
Your everlasting rivers speak
    Their dialect of yore.

Old Massachusetts wears it
　　Within her lordly crown,
And broad Ohio bears it
　　'Mid all her young renown;
Connecticut hath wreathed it
　　Where her quiet foliage waves,
And bold Kentucky breathes it hoarse,
　　Through all her ancient caves.

Wachusett hides its lingering voice
　　Within his rocky heart,
And Alleghany graves its tone
　　Throughout his lofty chart;
Monadnock on his forehead hoar
　　Both seal the sacred trust:
Your mountains build their monument,
　　Though ye destroy their dust.

LYDIA HUNTLEY SIGOURNEY

INVOCATION
FROM *John Brown's Body*

American muse, whose strong and diverse heart
So many men have tried to understand
But only made it smaller with their art,
Because you are as various as your land,

*   *   *   *   *

You are the buffalo-ghost, the broncho-ghost
With dollar-silver in your saddle-horn,
The cowboys riding in from Painted Post,
The Indian arrow in the Indian corn,

And you are the clipped velvet of the lawns
Where Shropshire grows from Massachusetts sods,
The grey Maine rocks—and the war-painted dawns
That break above the Garden of the Gods.

The prairie-schooners crawling toward the ore
And the cheap car, parked by the station-door.

Where the skyscrapers lift their foggy plumes
Of stranded smoke out of a stony mouth
You are that high stone and its arrogant fumes,
And you are ruined gardens in the South

And bleak New England farms, so winter-white
Even their roofs look lonely, and the deep
The middle grainland where the wind of night
Is like all blind earth sighing in her sleep.

A friend, an enemy, a sacred hag
With two tied oceans in her medicine-bag.

They tried to fit you with an English song
And clip your speech into the English tale.
But, even from the first, the words went wrong,
The catbird pecked away the nightingale.

The homesick men begot high-cheekboned things
Whose wit was whittled with a different sound
And Thames and all the rivers of the kings
Ran into Mississippi and were drowned.

STEPHEN VINCENT BENÉT

MAP OF MY COUNTRY

A map of my native country is all edges,
The shore touching sea, the easy impartial rivers
Splitting the local boundary lines, round hills in two
    townships,
Blue ponds interrupting the careful county shapes.
The Mississippi runs down the middle. Cape Cod. The
    Gulf.
Nebraska is on latitude forty. Kansas is west of Missouri.

When I was a child, I drew it, from memory,
A game in the schoolroom, naming the big cities right.

Cloud shadows were not shown, nor where winter whitens,
Nor the wide road the day's wind takes.
None of the tall letters told my grandfather's name.
Nothing said, Here they see in clear air a hundred miles.
Here they go to bed early. They fear snow here.

Oak trees and maple boughs I had seen on the long hill-
   sides
Changing color, and laurel, and bayberry, were never
   mapped.
Geography told only capitals and state lines.

I have come a long way using other men's maps for the
   turnings.
I have a long way to go.
It is time I drew the map again,
Spread with the broad colors of life, and words of my
   own
Saying, Here the people worked hard, and died for the
   wrong reasons.
Here wild strawberries tell the time of year.
I could not sleep, here, while bell-buoys beyond the surf
   rang.
Here trains passed in the night, crying of distance,
Calling to cities far away, listening for an answer.

On my own map of my own country
I shall show where there were never wars,
And plot the changed way I hear men speak in the west,
Words in the south slower, and food different.
Not the court-houses seen floodlighted at night from
   trains,
But the local stone built into housewalls,
And barns telling the traveler where he is
By the slant of the roof, the color of the paint.
Not monuments. Not the battlefields famous in school.
But Thoreau's pond, and Huckleberry Finn's island.
I shall name an unhistorical hill three boys climbed one
   morning.

Lines indicate my few journeys,
And the long way letters come from absent friends.

Forest is where green fern cooled me under the big trees.
Ocean is where I ran in the white drag of waves on white
     sand.
Music is what I heard in a country house while hearts
     broke,
Not knowing they were breaking, and Brahms wrote it.
All that I remember happened to me here.
This is the known world.
I shall make a star here for a man who died too young.
Here, and here, in gold, I shall mark two towns
Famous for nothing, except that I have been happy in
     them.

JOHN HOLMES

NEXT TO OF COURSE GOD AMERICA I

"next to of course god america i
love you land of the pilgrims' and so forth oh
say can you see by the dawn's early my
country 'tis of centuries come and go
and are no more what of it we should worry
in every language even deafanddumb
thy sons acclaim your glorious name by gorry
by jingo by gee by gosh by gum
why talk of beauty what could be more beautiful than these heroic happy dead
who rushed like lions to the roaring slaughter
they did not stop to think they died instead
then shall the voice of liberty be mute?"

He spoke.   And drank rapidly a glass of water.

E. E. CUMMINGS

BURNING IN THE NIGHT

Go seeker, if you will, throughout the land
And you will find us burning in the night.

There where the hackles of the Rocky Mountains
Blaze in the blank and naked radiance of the moon,
Go—
Make your resting-stool upon the highest peak.
Can you not see us now?

The continental wall juts sheer and flat,
Its huge black shadow on the plain,
And the plain sweeps out against the East,
Two thousand miles away.
The great snake that you see there
Is the Mississippi River.

Behold
The gem-strung towns and cities
Of the good, green East,
Flung like star-dust through the field of night.
That spreading constellation to the north
Is called Chicago,
And that giant wink that blazes in the moon
Is the pendant lake that it is built upon.
Beyond, close-set and dense as a clenched fist,
Are all the jeweled cities of the eastern seaboard.
There's Boston,
Ringed with the bracelet of its shining little towns,
And all the lights that sparkle
On the rocky indentations of New England.
Here, southward and a little to the west,
And yet still coasted to the sea,
Is our intensest ray,
The splintered firmament of the towered island
Of Manhattan.
Round about her, sown thick as grain,
Is the glitter of a hundred towns and cities.
The long chain of lights there
Is the necklace of Long Island and the Jersey shore.
Southward and inland, by a foot or two,
Behold the duller glare of Philadelphia.
Southward further still,
The twin constellations—Baltimore and Washington.

Westward, but still within the borders
Of the good, green East,
That nighttime glow and smolder of hell-fire
Is Pittsburgh.
Here, St. Louis, hot and humid
In the cornfield belly of the land,
And bedded on the mid-length coil and fringes
Of the snake.
There at the snake's mouth,
Southward six hundred miles or so,
You see the jeweled crescent of old New Orleans,
Here, west and south again,
You see the gemmy glitter
Of the cities on the Texas border.

Turn now, seeker,
On your resting-stool atop the Rocky Mountains,
And look another thousand miles or so
Across moon-blazing fiend-worlds of the Painted Desert
And beyond Sierra's ridge.
That magic congeries of lights
There to the west,
Ringed like a studded belt
Around the magic setting of its lovely harbor,
Is the fabled town of San Francisco.
Below it, Los Angeles
And all the cities of the California shore.
A thousand miles to north and west,
The sparkling towns of Oregon and Washington.

Observe the whole of it,
Survey it as you might survey a field.

Make it your garden, seeker,
Or your backyard patch.
Be at ease in it.
It's your oyster—yours to open if you will.
Don't be frightened,
It's not so big now,
When your footstool is the Rocky Mountains.
Reach out
And dip a hatful of cold water
From Lake Michigan.
Drink it—we've tried it—
You'll not find it bad.
Take your shoes off
And work your toes down in the river oozes
Of the Mississippi bottom—
It's very refreshing
On a hot night in the summertime.

Help yourself to a bunch of Concord grapes
Up there in northern New York State—
They're getting good now.
Or raid that watermelon patch
Down there in Georgia.
Or, if you like, you can try the Rockyfords
Here at your elbow, in Colorado.
Just make yourself at home,
Refresh yourself, get the feel of things,
Adjust your sights, and get the scale.
It's your pasture now, and it's not so big—
Only three thousand miles from east to west,
Only two thousand miles from north to south—
But all between,

Where ten thousand points of light
Prick out the cities, towns, and villages,
There, seeker,
You will find us burning in the night.

*   *   *   *   *

THOMAS WOLFE

SHINE, REPUBLIC

The quality of these trees, green height; of the sky, shin-
        ing, of water, a clear flow; of the rock, hardness
And reticence: each is noble in its quality. The love of
        freedom has been the quality of Western man.

There is a stubborn torch that flames from Marathon to
        Concord, its dangerous beauty binding three ages
Into one time; the waves of barbarism and civilization
        have eclipsed but have never quenched it.

For the Greeks the love of beauty, for Rome of ruling;
        for the present age the passionate love of discovery;
But in one noble passion we are one; and Washington,
        Luther, Tacitus, Aeschylus, one kind of man.

And you, America, that passion made you. You were not
        born to prosperity, you were born to love freedom.
You did not say "en masse," you said "independence."
        But we cannot have all the luxuries and freedom
        also.

Freedom is poor and laborious; that torch is not safe but
        hungry, and often requires blood for its fuel.

You will tame it against it burn too clearly, you will hood
    it like a kept hawk, you will perch it on the wrist
    of Caesar.

But keep the tradition, conserve the forms, the observ-
    ances, keep the spot sore. Be great, carve deep your
    heel-marks.
The states of the next age will no doubt remember you,
    and edge their love of freedom with contempt of
    luxury.

ROBINSON JEFFERS

TRAVELING AMERICA

Traveling America, I am England-haunted.
    I seek new landscapes out of the window of the train,
But wherever I look, an England enlarged, transplanted,
    Springs to my sight, and carries me home again.

The clapboard house in a Massachusetts village
    Is a weatherboard house in Essex. From both, men sail
To plow their lives away in a dangerous tillage;
    In both, wives lie uneasy, an ear on the gale.

The Pennsylvania meadows are green and quiet
    As Penn's own meadows three thousand miles away;
The cattle browse, and the honeysuckles riot,
    And the streams run slow, and slow men cart the hay.

In Chesapeake Bay the woods come down to the water,
    Feathery-soft in the moonlight as funeral plumes:

I think of a small mother with a well-grown daughter,
    And remember the Devon coast and the wooded combes.

The Shenandoah Valley, the Blue Ridge lying
    Beyond it, the sound of crickets and whippoorwills—
This is the valley of Avon, with plovers crying,
    And daylight dying over the Malvern Hills.

Southward. Kentucky. Small fields, steep and stony;
    Patient eyes staring from a rickety shack.
(I've seen those eyes in Scotland, and the one cow bony,
    And the stunted crops, raised with a breaking back.)

Mobile. Biloxi. Rose-pink water-mallows
    Along the Gulf, in the marshes of Pontchartrain.
(The marshes of Kent are smaller; their creeks run shallow;
    Their mallow-blooms are paler, and wet with rain.)

The grazing lands . . . It is only the size that varies.
    Mind's eye sees color and shape, but has no scale:
It can gather the length and breadth of Nebraska's prairies
    On the fells of Yorkshire, hard by Arkendale.

The orchards of Michigan and Minnesota
    Are Hereford apple-orchards in blossomtime;
And, climbing the long Black Hills of South Dakota,
    It is still the Monadhliath that I climb.

But here, in the Southwest, opening my eyes on
    Vermilion mesas rising from painted sands,
I have found at last a land with a new horizon,
    A land which holds no echoes of other lands.

Here are cactus and thorn, with nightmare flowers;
    Basalt and gypsum; trees long turned to stone.
Over the dried arroyo the red cliff towers:
    Here is nothing familiar, nothing known.

Silence, and sun, and sand. The lizards flicker.
    Ghostly and restless rolls the tumbleweed.
The eyes that gaze from the scattered huts of wicker
    Are the secret eyes of an ancient and secret breed.

This is a country of dream, a world enchanted,
    Improbable, fantastic, a wild release.
Here, and here alone, I can walk unhaunted.
    I shall stay here long. Strangeness, at last, brings peace.

JAN STRUTHER

CARRY ME BACK

The big blue-jean, the summer-bored boy next door,
Has been marching through Georgia all afternoon.
Tramp, tramp, tramp on the piano, his fists have trod
The vineyard where my grapes of wrath are stored.
He has brought Johnny marching home again, again,
And tented on the old camp ground tonight once more.
I am a captive audience, neighbor slave to noise.

One-fingered, he wanders way down the Suwanee River,
Where his heart, like mine, that's where it's turning
Ever. He asks the key of F, C, or G to carry him back.
Carry me back to ole Virginny (now it's both hands)
Where the corn and taters grow, beyond this hot
Suburban house, family, no school, no job, no fun.

21

Back to where I used to banjo my way back to,
Andersonville, Gettysburg, the decks of the *Monitor*.
Gone are the days, but we hear the voices calling.

By way of Brady's camera, when I was this boy's age,
I wanted to creep near Lincoln and that chin-beard,
Through my uncle's stereopticon to Grant's staff tent,
And hear that posed group break it up, and talk,
Lincoln to Brady, Grant to Lincoln, the wrinkled generals,
Belted and bewhiskered, to one another and the dog.

I'd be there in a forage-cap, with a long bayonet
Fixed to my long rifle, and my own cartridge-belt.
I'd stand guard, a sentry, in the timbered trenches,
Those snug play-places in a home-war that made sad songs.
Old Black Joe. Old Abe Lincoln. Old Virginny.
Old camp ground. Old boy next door, and old me.

JOHN HOLMES

THE PINTA, THE NINA
AND THE SANTA MARIA; AND MANY
OTHER CARGOES OF LIGHT

America
I
carry
you
around   a
with   poem
me   growing   the
the   expanding   way
way   like   eloquence
Buddha   a   carries
carried   galaxy   hope,
a   the   faith,
grain   way   and
of sand   a   the
the   firefly   4th
way   carries   of
Columbus   a   July.
carried   galaxy
a   the
compass   way
the way   Faulkner
Whitman   carries
carried   eloquence

JOHN TAGLIABUE

23

ℰAGLE PLAIN

The American eagle is not aware he is
the American eagle. He is never tempted
to look modest.

When orators advertise the American eagle's
virtues, the American eagle is not listening.
This is his virtue.

He is somewhere else, he is mountains away
but even if he were near he would never
make an audience.

The American eagle never says he will serve
if drafted, will dutifully serve, etc. He is
not at our service.

If we have honored him we have honored one
who unequivocally honors himself by
overlooking us.

He does not know the meaning of magnificent.
Perhaps we do not altogether either
who cannot touch him.

ROBERT FRANCIS

THE BIRDS OF AMERICA

Said the Birds of America:
   quak quek quark quark, hoo hoo
   rarrp rarrp, gogogogock
   feebee, cheep cheep, kakakaaa
   coo ahh, choo eee, coo coo!

And what is the meaning of that?
said the solemn Birdcage Maker.

O nothing at all, said the Old Turkey,
we just enjoy the noise.

Why not do something that makes some sense?
said the serious Birdcage Man.

   We do, we do, all there is to do,
said the Eagle, the Lark, and the others:
   We eat and sleep and move about
   and watch what's going on.
   We mate and nest and sit and hatch
   and watch the young get on.
   We hunt and preen and sing and wash,
   we take long journeys and local jaunts
   or simply sit about and scratch
   and watch what's going on.

But that's quite pointless! said the Birdcage Man,
You'll never get anywhere that way.

Maybe, said the Magpie. Yet when this continent began
we birds were the only two-legged creatures
and we're still very much around.

What's more, the Woodpecker added,
everything man knows he learned from us birds
but he's never enjoyed it as much.

The Cagemaker scoffed: What could I learn from you?

To do, to do, all there is to do,
said the Heron, the Crow, and the others:
    To eat and sleep and move about
    and watch what's going on.
    To mate and nest and sit and hatch
    and watch the young get on.
    To hunt and preen and sing and wash,
    to take long journeys and local jaunts
    or simply sit about and scratch
    and watch what's going on.

O that's absurd! said the Birdcage Maker,
Don't you know the real meaning of life?

Of course we do, said the Birds of America:
    quak quek quark quark, hoo hoo
    rarrp rarrp, gogogogock
    feebee, cheep cheep, kakakaaa
    coo ahh, choo eee, coo coo!

JAMES BROUGHTON

LOVE SONG

I know not how to speak to thee, girl (damselle?),
Not how to begin to begin with thee to commune
In all your lazy lingos, oh my America!
Or say to you, honey (light of my life, doll),
That on you I'm sweet.

America, child,
Thou of the silken thighs and purple sage brush,
How, huh, does it fare with thee?
Art thou Wyoming, Memphis? Yare, art thou?
What dost thy lover durst, what idiom suffer
To the apple be
Of your eye?

Your suitors grow old, old, their lyrics sodden
And their passions fizz in the soft, westering rhetoric.
But you, oh Nik-Nak-Nookie, Dairie Queene,
From all your Southern Cal to Keep Maine Green,
You still—or so thou tellest me?—mean?

REED WHITTEMORE

SIGNATURES

My fathers wrote their names in sweat
On forest and on farming land.
Each ax and plowshare, hard to get,
Spelled out a purpose in their hand.

My brothers wrote their names in steel.
Huge buildings rose at their desire;
They hitched explosion to a wheel
And harnessed lightning to a wire.

On air my children wrought their will.
Gaily they rode from cloud to cloud,
And if they dropped destruction, still
They liked their writing and were proud.

Their children sign their names in yet
More grimly catastrophic terms—
An elemental alphabet
Of splintered atom, stalking germs.

CANDACE THURBER STEVENSON

THE GIFT OUTRIGHT

The land was ours before we were the land's.
She was our land more than a hundred years
Before we were her people. She was ours
In Massachusetts, in Virginia,
But we were England's, still colonials,
Possessing what we still were unpossessed by,
Possessed by what we now no more possessed.
Something we were withholding left us weak
Until we found out that it was ourselves
We were withholding from our land of living
And forthwith found salvation in surrender.
Such as we were we gave ourselves outright
(The deed of gift was many deeds of war)
To the land vaguely realizing westward,
But still unstoried, artless, unenhanced,
Such as she was, such as she would become.

ROBERT FROST

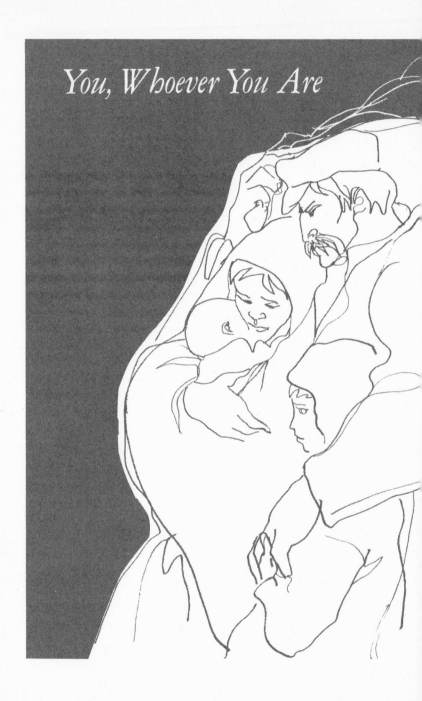

You, Whoever You Are

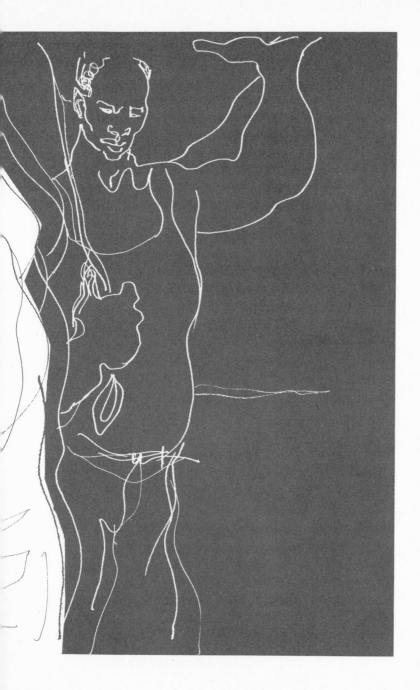

You, whoever you are! . . .
All you continentals of Asia, Africa, Europe, Aus-
    tralia, indifferent of place!

        *   *   *   *   *

All you each and everywhere whom I specify not,
    but include just the same!
Health to you! good will to you all, from me and
    America sent!

                        —WALT WHITMAN

ALL ONE PEOPLE

What did Hiamovi, the red man, Chief of the Cheyennes
 have?
To a great chief at Washington and to a chief of peoples
 across the waters, Hiamovi spoke:
"There are birds of many colors—red, blue, green, yellow,
Yet it is all one bird.
There are horses of many colors—brown, black, yellow,
 white,
Yet it is all one horse.
So cattle, so all living things, animals, flowers, trees.
So men in this land, where once were only Indians, are
 now men of many colors—white, black, yellow, red.
Yet all one people.
That this should come to pass was in the heart of the
 Great Mystery.
It is right thus—and everywhere there shall be peace."
Thus Hiamovi, out of a tarnished and weatherworn heart
 of old gold, out of a living dawn gold.

CARL SANDBURG

from THE COMING AMERICAN

Bring me men to match my mountains,
 Bring me men to match my plains . . .
Bring me men to match my prairies,
 Men to match my inland seas,
Men whose thoughts shall pave a highway
 Up to ampler destinies,

Pioneers to clear thought's marshlands,
    And to cleanse old error's fen;
Bring me men to match my mountains—
    Bring me men!

Bring me men to match my forests,
    Strong to fight the storm and blast,
Branching toward the skyey future,
    Rooted in the fertile past.
Bring me men to match my valleys,
    Tolerant of sun and snow,
Men within whose fruitful purpose
    Time's consummate blooms shall grow,
Men to tame the tigerish instincts
    Of the lair and cave and den,
Cleanse the dragon slime of nature—
    Bring me men!

Bring me men to match my rivers,
    Continent cleavers, flowing free,
Drawn by the eternal madness,
    To be mingled with the sea;
Men of oceanic impulse,
    Men whose moral currents sweep
Toward the wide, infolding ocean
    Of an undiscovered deep;
Men who feel the strong pulsation
    Of the central sea, and then
Time their currents by its earth throb—
    Bring me men!

SAM WALTER FOSS

from A NATION'S STRENGTH

Not gold, but only man can make
   A people great and strong;
Men who, for truth and honor's sake,
   Stand fast and suffer long.

Brave men who work while others sleep,
   Who dare while others fly—
They build a nation's pillar's deep
   And lift them to the sky.

RALPH WALDO EMERSON

IMMIGRANTS

"These foreigners with strange and avid faces
Crowding our shores, marring our pleasant places,
They must be curbed. . . ." So mused King Powhatan,
Hundred per cent, red-blood American.

NANCY BYRD TURNER

INDIANS

Margaret mentioned Indians,
And I began to think about Indians—

Indians once living
Where now we are living—

And I thought how little I know
About Indians. Oh, I know

What I have heard. Not much,
When I think how much

I wonder about them,
When a mere mention of them,

Indians, starts me. I
Think of their wigwams. I

Think of canoes. I think
Of quick arrows. I think

Of things Indian. And still
I think of their bright, still

Summers, when these hills
And meadows on these hills

Shone in the morning
Suns before this morning.

JOHN FANDEL

THE NAVAJO

Lean and tall and stringy are the Navajo,
workers in silver and the turquoise, herders of flocks,
their sheep and goats cover the hills like smooth rocks.

They wear velvet shirts, they are proud, they go
through the sage, upright on thin bright horses,
their speech is low.
At their necks they gather the black smooth cataract of
     their locks,
quick are their eyes and bright as the eyes of a fox.
You may pass close by their encampments and never
     know.

ELIZABETH COATSWORTH

A SONG OF GREATNESS
From the Chippewa

When I hear the old men
Telling of heroes,
Telling of great deeds
Of ancient days,
When I hear that telling
Then I think within me
I too am one of these.

When I hear the people
Praising great ones,
Then I know that I too
Shall be esteemed,
I too when my time comes
Shall do mightily.

MARY AUSTIN

CIRCLES

The white man drew a small circle in the sand and told
     the red man,
"This is what the Indian knows,"
And drawing a big circle around the small one,
"This is what the white man knows."

The Indian took the stick
And swept an immense ring around both circles:
"This is where the white man and the red man know
     nothing."

CARL SANDBURG

A FELLER I KNOW

His name it is Pedro-Pablo-Ignacio-Juan-
Francesco García y Gabaldon,
But the fellers call him Pete;
His folks belong to the Conquistadores
And he lives at the end of our street.

His father's father's great-grandfather
Was friends with the King of Spain
And his father peddles hot tamales
From here to Acequia-Madre Lane.

And Pete knows every one of the signs
For things that are lucky to do,
A charm to say for things that are lost,
And roots that are good to chew.

Evenings we go to Pedro's house
When there's firelight and rain
To hear of the Indians his grandfather fought
When they first came over from Spain.

And how De Vargas with swords and spurs
Came riding down our street,
And Pedro's mother gives us cakes
That are strange and spicey and sweet.

And we hear of gold that is buried and lost
On ranches they used to own,
And all us fellers think a lot
Of Pedro-Pablo-Ignacio-Juan-
Francesco García y Gabaldon.

MARY AUSTIN

MY NAME WAS LEGION

My name was legion,
   I came in every slave ship to the Colonies,
      In every slave ship.

Mine was the long horror of the middle passage,
The cruel kiss of the whip, the darkness, the burden of
      chains.
Mine the stench of the hold, the groans of the dying.
Mine the queasy lurch of the ship, the hungry roar of the
      sea.
Mine the long, long horror and the hope of death,
   But still I endured.

I came in every slave ship to the Colonies,
  Through the loss of my own freedom
    To build a world for the free.

HILDEGARDE HOYT SWIFT

I CAME TO THE NEW WORLD EMPTY-HANDED

I came to the New World empty-handed,
  A despised thing, to be used and broken,
Yet I brought immeasurable gifts.
I brought the gentleness of the Bantu,
  The Dahomian's arrogance and courage.
I brought devotion—and wisdom—
  The knowledge of jungle ways and jungle rhythms,
  Wind-magic and moon-magic,
The knowledge of communion with the mystery men call
    God.

I stood in the water of the rice fields,
  I bent beneath the sun of the cotton lands,
I mined the ore hidden in the earth,
  I laid the ties of the railroads,
I swung the axes and cleared the forests
  And served in the white man's kitchen.

I built your world, oh, white man, but in the building
  It became mine too.

HILDEGARDE HOYT SWIFT

EUROPE AND AMERICA

My father brought the emigrant bundle
of desperation and worn threads,
that in anxiety as he stumbles
tumble out distractedly;
while I am bedded upon soft green money
that grows like grass. Thus,
between my father who lives on a bed of anguish
for his daily bread, and I who tear money
at leisure by the roots,
where I lie in sun or shade,
a vast continent of breezes, storms to him,
shadows, darkness to him, small lakes,
difficult channels to him, and hills,
mountains to him, lie between us.

My father comes of a hell
where bread and man have been kneaded
and baked together. You have heard the scream
as the knife fell; while I have slept
as guns pounded on the shore.

DAVID IGNATOW

FISH CRIER

I know a Jew fish crier down on Maxwell Street, with a
    voice like a north wind blowing over corn stubble in
    January.
He dangles herring before prospective customers evincing
    a joy identical with that of Pavlova dancing.
His face is that of a man terribly glad to be selling fish,
    terribly glad that God made fish, and customers to
    whom he may call his wares from a pushcart.

CARL SANDBURG

CLINTON SOUTH OF POLK

I wander down on Clinton street south of Polk
And listen to the voices of Italian children quarreling.
It is a cataract of coloratura
And I could sleep to their musical threats and accusations.

CARL SANDBURG

IRISH GRANDMOTHER

Great-grandmother talks by the hour to me
Of a little cottage in Ballybree,
Of whitewashed walls and a roof of thatch
And a gay green ribbon that raised the latch.

Great-grandmother tells of a wee boreen,
With fern and shamrock, moisty-green,
Of a thrush that sang in a hawthorn bough,
Of an old furze patch, and a Kerry cow.

Great-grandmother speaks of the little folk,
Of blazing peat, with its tangy smoke,
Of quaint tall cups they used for tea,
When she was a child in Ballybree.

KATHERINE EDELMAN

I HEAR AMERICA GRIPING

Luther B—— stepped from his air-conditioned house
    Directly into his air-conditioned car.
He drove, tight-windowed, to his air-conditioned office.
    Returning, he stopped in an air-conditioned bar,
And spent the evening in an air-conditioned movie.
    "The thing," he said, "that seems to me most unfair—
I must walk unprotected from parking-place to street
        door.
    Everything is air-conditioned except the air."

MORRIS BISHOP

I HEAR AMERICA SINGING

I hear America singing, the varied carols I hear,
Those of mechanics, each one singing his as it should
     be blithe and strong,
The carpenter singing his as he measures his plank or
     beam,
The mason singing his as he makes ready for work, or
     leaves off work,
The boatman singing what belongs to him in his boat, the
     deckhand singing on the steamboat deck,
The shoemaker singing as he sits on his bench, the hatter
     singing as he stands,
The woodcutter's song, the plowboy's on his way in the
     morning, or at noon intermission or at sundown,
The delicious singing of the mother, or of the young wife
     at work, or of the girl sewing or washing,
Each singing what belongs to him or her and to none
     else,
The day what belongs to the day—at night the party of
     young fellows, robust, friendly,
Singing with open mouths their strong melodious songs.

WALT WHITMAN

AMERICANS ARE AFRAID OF LIZARDS

My American host in Madras in his moist air-conditioned
    apartment
Spotted a lizard and yelled for a servant to kill it, kill it!
And a beautifully turbaned, silent and grinning Hindu,
    beautifully barefooted, beautifully servant,
Rushed in with a towel and pretending to smack it to
    death
Impounded it gently and carried it off to the gorgeous
    and sweating garden
To let it go.

In earlier years, on my first trip to the tropics,
I screamed at a lizard on my pillow,
And the fat Tahitian lady stuffed it in her hand
And grinned toothlessly and pointed to the ceiling
Frescoed with twenty or thirty of the pretty beasts
All vividly flicking their tongues at mosquitoes,
Or playing at making designs.

KARL SHAPIRO

YOU'VE GOT TO BE TAUGHT

You've got to be taught to hate and fear,
You've got to be taught from year to year,
It's got to be drummed in your dear little ear—
You've got to be carefully taught!

You've got to be taught to be afraid
Of people whose eyes are oddly made,
And people whose skin is a different shade—
You've got to be carefully taught.

You've got to be taught before it's too late,
Before you are six or seven or eight,
To hate all the people your relatives hate—
You've got to be carefully taught!
You've got to be carefully taught!

OSCAR HAMMERSTEIN II

DAYBREAK IN ALABAMA

When I get to be a composer
I'm gonna write me some music about
Daybreak in Alabama
And I'm gonna put the purtiest songs in it
Rising out of the ground like a swamp mist
And falling out of heaven like soft dew.
I'm gonna put some tall tall trees in it
And the scent of pine needles
And the smell of red clay after rain
And the long red necks
And poppy colored faces
And big brown arms
And the field daisy eyes
Of black and white black white black people
And I'm gonna put white hands
And black hands and brown and yellow hands
And red clay earth hands in it
Touching everybody with kind fingers
And touching each other natural as dew
In that dawn of music when I
Get to be a composer
And write about daybreak
In Alabama.

LANGSTON HUGHES

ALABAMA EARTH
(At Booker Washington's Grave)

Deep in Alabama earth
His buried body lies—
But higher than the singing pines
And taller than the skies
And out of Alabama earth
To all the world there goes
The truth a simple heart has held
And the strength a strong hand knows,
While over Alabama earth
These words are gently spoken:
Serve—and hate will die unborn.
Love—and chains are broken.

LANGSTON HUGHES

YOU, WHOEVER YOU ARE

You, whoever you are! . . .

All you continentals of Asia, Africa, Europe, Australia,
   indifferent of place!
All you on the numberless islands of the archipelagoes
   of the sea!
All you of centuries hence when you listen to me!
All you each and everywhere whom I specify not, but
   include just the same!
Health to you! good will to you all, from me and Amer-
   ica sent!
Each of us is inevitable,
Each of us is limitless—each of us with his or her right
   upon the earth,
Each of us allow'd the eternal purports of the earth,
Each of us here as divinely as any is here.

WALT WHITMAN

Conceived in Liberty

. . . our fathers brought forth upon
this continent a new nation, conceived in liberty,
and dedicated to the proposition that all men
are created equal.

—ABRAHAM LINCOLN

COLUMBUS

How in Heaven's name did Columbus get over
    Is a pure wonder to me, I protest;
Cabot, and Raleigh too, that well-read rover,
    Frobisher, Dampier, Drake, and the rest.
        Bad enough all the same,
        For them that after came,
        But, in great Heaven's name,
        How *he* should ever think
        That on the other brink
Of this wild waste, terra firma should be,
Is a pure wonder, I must say, to me.

How a man ever should hope to get thither,
    E'en if he knew that there was another side;
But to suppose he should come any whither,
    Sailing straight on into chaos untried,—
        In spite of the motion
        Across the whole ocean,
        To stick to the notion
        That in some nook or bend
        Of a sea without end
He should find North and South America,
Was a pure madness, indeed I must say.

What if wise men had, as far back as Ptolemy,
    Judged that the earth like an orange was round,
None of them ever said, "Come along, follow me,
    Sail to the West and the East will be found."
        Many a day before
        Even they'd come ashore,

Sadder and wiser men,
They'd have turned back again;
And that *he* did not, but did cross the sea,
Is a pure wonder, I must say, to me.

ARTHUR HUGH CLOUGH

THERE WAS AN INDIAN

There was an Indian, who had known no change,
    Who strayed content along a sunlit beach
Gathering shells. He heard a sudden strange
    Commingled noise; looked up; and gasped for speech.
For in the bay, where nothing was before,
    Moved on the sea, by magic, huge canoes,
With bellying cloth on poles, and not one oar,
    And fluttering colored signs and clambering crews.

And he, in fear, this naked man alone,
    His fallen hands forgetting all their shells,
His lips gone pale, knelt low behind a stone,
    And stared, and saw, and did not understand,
Columbus's doom-burdened caravels
    Slant to the shore, and all their seamen land.

J. C. SQUIRE

POCAHONTAS

Wearied arm and broken sword
  Wage in vain the desperate fight;
Round him press a countless horde,
  He is but a single knight.
Hark! a cry of triumph shrill
  Through the wilderness resounds,
  As, with twenty bleeding wounds,
Sinks the warrior, fighting still.

Now they heap the funeral pyre,
  And the torch of death they light;
Ah! 'tis hard to die by fire!
  Who will shield the captive knight?
Round the stake with fiendish cry
  Wheel and dance the savage crowd,
  Cold the victim's mien and proud,
And his breast is bared to die.

Who will shield the fearless heart?
  Who avert the murderous blade?
From the throng with sudden start
  See, there springs an Indian maid.
Quick she stands before the knight:
  "Loose the chain, unbind the ring!
  I am daughter of the king,
And I claim the Indian right!"

Dauntlessly aside she slings
   Lifted axe and thirsty knife;
Fondly to his heart she clings,
   And her bosom guards his life!
In the woods of Powhatan,
   Still 'tis told by Indian fires
   How a daughter of their sires
Saved a captive Englishman.

WILLIAM MAKEPEACE THACKERAY

SOUTHERN SHIPS AND SETTLERS
1606–1732

O, where are you going, "Goodspeed" and "Discovery"?
With meek "Susan Constant" to make up the three?
We're going to settle the wilds of Virginia,
For gold and adventure we're crossing the sea.

And what will you find there? Starvation and fever.
We'll eat of the adder and quarrel and rail.
All but sixty shall die of the first seven hundred,
But a nation begins with the voyage we sail.

O, what are you doing, my handsome Lord Baltimore?
Where are you sending your "Ark" and your "Dove"?
I'm sending them over the ocean to Maryland
To build up a refuse for people I love.

Both Catholic and Protestant there may find harbor,
Though I am a Catholic by creed and by prayer.
The South is Virginia, the North is New England
I'll go in the middle and plant my folk there.

O, what do you seek, "Carolina" and "Albemarle,"
Now the Stuarts are up and the Roundheads are down?
We'll seek and we'll find, to the South of Virginia,
A site by two rivers and name it Charles Town.

And, in South Carolina, the cockfighting planters
Will dance with their belles by a tropical star.
And, in North Carolina, the sturdy Scotch-Irish
Will prove at King's Mountain the metal they are.

O, what are you dreaming, cock-hatted James Oglethorpe?
And who are the people you take in the "Anne"?
They're poor English debtors whom hard laws imprison,
And poor, distressed Protestants, fleeing a ban.

I'll settle them pleasantly on the Savannah,
With Germans and Highlanders, thrifty and strong.
They shall eat Georgia peaches in huts of palmetto,
And their land shall be fertile, their days shall be long.

We're the barques and the sailors, the bread on the waters,
The seed that was planted and grew to be tall,
And the South was first won by our toils and our dangers,
So remember our journey. Remember us all.

ROSEMARY and STEPHEN VINCENT BENÉT

THE NEW WORLD

There was a strange and unknown race,
Great, gaunt ghost from the verge of time,
The first to settle and dig a place
Deep in the rich American earth,
To beat out metal and fashion clay—
These left their bones in a beast-shaped mound

*   *   *   *   *

And the wind reëchoed night and day
With the dark god's chant and the arrow's sound.

*   *   *   *   *

The Spaniard came and the Spanish horse
Neighed in the never-trampled plain,
Cruel-lipped men with a single course—
Gold! cried their hearts, and their armor glittered
Gold! while they burned the scanty grain
And in the high city of the god
Tore his temple down and littered
The human-scavenged streets with dead.
The only gold they found was the yellow
Curse of fever in the head
And the fiery sun's enormous bellow.
But they brought their god, and the slow attrition
Of time has left us yet the mellow
Walls of the 'dobe-builded mission.

*   *   *   *   *

The French came for the beaver fur
And brought the Crucifix—the Mass
Was said in the wilderness, the stir
Of hawks in the trees, of wolves in the grass
Muffling the Latin, while the priest

58

Dipped his hand in the common pot
And slept with the dogs, to find his least
Pain in watching his sick feet rot
In the neck-deep snow. They took the land
And gave it to God with sword and prayer
While the Indian found the white man's hand
Double—his saviour and his slayer.

* * * * *

The English armies marched and shattered
The frail French power, and America fought
The English till the redcoats scattered
From Maine to Georgia, and there was brought
Out of the ripping pain of war
A new world nation . . . .

PAUL ENGLE

CONQUEST

The axe has cut the forest down,
the laboring ox has smoothed all clear,
apples now grow where pine trees stood,
and slow cows graze instead of deer.

Where Indian fires once raised their smoke
the chimneys of a farmhouse stand,
and cocks crow barnyard challenges
to dawns that once saw savage land.

The axe, the plow, the binding wall,
by these the wilderness is tamed,
by these the white man's will is wrought,
the rivers bridged, and new towns named.

ELIZABETH COATSWORTH

THE PATH OF THE PADRES

Across a sage-grown upland
    Once, on a summer day,
I found an old path, winding
    Its long-forgotten way,
Half-hidden by tall grasses
    That surged up from the vale
And nodded heads of silver
    Along the lonely trail.

Long, long ago, the padres
    With weary feet, and slow,
Marked out this earliest highway
    And showed the way to go;
From Mission unto Mission
    Through all the golden land,
Bright with the glow of poppies
    That bloomed on every hand.

The padres long are sleeping
    At peace beneath the sod,
And a more stately highway
    Outlines the way they trod;

But ah—across the uplands
    And over the brown hill,
The little path, forgotten,
    Winds on in beauty still.

EDITH D. OSBORNE

CONCORD HYMN

By the rude bridge that arched the flood,
    Their flag to April's breeze unfurled,
Here once the embattled farmers stood,
    And fired the shot heard round the world.

The foe long since in silence slept;
    Alike the conqueror silent sleeps;
And Time the ruined bridge has swept
    Down the dark stream which seaward creeps.

On this green bank, by this soft stream,
    We set today a votive stone;
That memory may their deeds redeem,
    When, like our sires, our sons are gone.

Spirit that made those heroes dare
    To die, and leave their children free,
Bid time and nature gently spare
    The shaft we raise to them and thee.

RALPH WALDO EMERSON

PROPHECY IN FLAME

Grandfather wrote from Valley Forge,
"My dear, I miss you; times are harder;
The cheeses sent from home received,
A fine addition to our larder."

Grandfather wrote, "The volunteers
Are leaving—going home for haying;
We lose militia day by day;
But still a few of us are staying."

Grandfather wrote, "Last night I gave
My blanket to a soldier who
Was wrapped in rags; Phoebe, my dear,
The nights are cold. I dream of you."

Grandfather wrote, "That grand old man
Who bears us up seems not to tire;
I speak of General Washington,
Who last night shared with us his fire."

Grandfather dipped his quill and wrote,
Sanded and sealed his letter; sent it
Off with a splash of sealing wax,
Thinking of her for whom he meant it,

Nor dreamed that soldiers hungering here
Would feed a nation's new desire,
And men unborn would warm themselves
At that same small, fierce-flickering fire.

FRANCES MINTURN HOWARD

MY COUNTRY NEED NOT
CHANGE HER GOWN

My country need not change her gown,
Her triple suit as sweet
As when 'twas cut at Lexington,
And first pronounced "a fit."

Great Britain disapproves "the stars";
Disparagement discreet,—
There's something in their attitude
That taunts her bayonet.

EMILY DICKINSON

DANIEL BOONE
1735–1820

When Daniel Boone goes by, at night,
The phantom deer arise
And all lost, wild America
Is burning in their eyes.

ROSEMARY and STEPHEN VINCENT BENÉT

WALTHENA
Kentucky, c. 1785

I turned my back when in the pot they tossed
My pewter spoons, to mold as shot for guns.
My mother owned a shelf of shining spoons and plates;—
Can we have none but home-made wooden ones,
    Just handmade wooden ones?

I asked your father once if we might have
Crock plates to set our table. He said, "No,"
They dulled men's knives. So we must eat from plates
    of wood,
To keep knife-blades well sharped against the foe,
    The ever-lurking foe.

Back home each Saturday my mother made
White candles, clean and straight. But out west here
Your father, laughing, scorns to make a candle mold,
When we have fatty pine-knots always near,
    Pine-knots and greasy bear-dips always near.

If I could hope some day to own a gown
Of smooth, fine store-cloth, little would I care
That I have only homespun linsey-woolsey now,
And shapeless shoepacks stiffed with moss to wear,
    Coarse, shapeless clothes to wear.

But though I could not own a pewter spoon nor store-
    cloth dress,
I snatched at least some beauty for my brood.
When pappy gave the boys their names, and I the girls,
He gave man-names that seemed like puncheons rude,
    Ax-hewn puncheons rude.

But I chose names for loveliness alone.
Fair-Anna is a spoon of silver bright,
Lizelle a silken gown, Morene a china bowl,
And you, Walthena, are a candle white,
    A tall, smooth candle white,
        Walthena.

ELISABETH PECK

65

THE ERIE CANAL

I've got a mule, her name is Sal,
Fifteen years on the Erie Canal.
She's a good old worker and a good old pal,
Fifteen years on the Erie Canal.
We've hauled some barges in our day,
Filled with lumber, coal, and hay.
And every inch of the way I know
From Albany to Buffalo.

Low bridge, everybody down!
Low bridge, for we're comin' to a town!
You can always tell your neighbor, can always tell your
        pal,
If you've ever navigated on the Erie Canal.

We'd better look for a job, old gal,
Fifteen years on the Erie Canal.
You bet your life I wouldn't part with Sal,
Fifteen years on the Erie Canal.
Giddap there, Sal, we've passed that lock,
We'll make Rome 'fore six o'clock,
So one more trip and then we'll go
Right straight back to Buffalo.

Low bridge, everybody down!
Low bridge, for we're comin' to a town!
You can always tell your neighbor, can always tell your
        pal,
If you've ever navigated on the Erie Canal.

Where would I be if I lost my pal?
Fifteen years on the Erie Canal.
Oh, I'd like to see a mule as good as Sal,
Fifteen years on the Erie Canal.
A friend of mine once got her sore,
Now he's got a broken jaw,
'Cause she let fly with her iron toe
And kicked him into Buffalo.

Low bridge, everybody down!
Low bridge, for we're comin' to a town!
You can always tell your neighbor, can always tell your
    pal,
If you've ever navigated on the Erie Canal.

AUTHOR UNKNOWN

ANDREW JACKSON

He was a man as hot as whiskey.
He was a man whose word was good.
He was a man whose hate was risky—
    Andrew Jackson—hickory wood!

He was in love with love and glory:
His hopes were prospered, but at a price—
The bandying of the ugly story
    He'd had to marry his Rachel twice.

Hot he was and a hasty suitor,
But if he sinned he was poor at sin.
She was plain as a spoon of pewter,
    Plain and good as a safety pin.

Andrew Jackson, man of honor,
Held her name like he held his head.
He stopped a bullet for slurs upon her.
    All his life he carried lead.

All his life wherever he went he
Wore the scar of a pistol shot—
Along with others he had in plenty.
    Hickory wood is hard to rot.

Hard to rot and a fiery fuel—
When faith and freedom both burned dim,
He stood his guns as he fought a duel,
    And heartened others to stand with him.

With any man who was good at sighting,
No ally but the thief Lafitte,
And no campaigns but Indian fighting—
    He brought the British to black defeat.

The odds against him were more than double.
His gunmounts sank like a heart that fails,
Sank in mud and the frosty stubble—
    So he set his cannon on cotton bales.

And over the cane and the silver sedges—
The redcoats' coats were as red as flame—
In a hundred rows like a hundred hedges,
    The bayonets of the British came.

The smoke of his cannon rolled and scattered
Like bursting flowers, like cotton blooms.
Like teeth from a comb the red ranks shattered,
    While water lifted in yellow plumes.

White and red on the silver carpet,
Scarlet tunics by crossbelts crossed,
They fell and died—and a flood of scarlet
    Covered over the field of frost.

He was a man whose hand was steady.
He was a man whose aim was good.
He was a man whose guns were ready—
    Andrew Jackson—hickory wood!

MARTHA KELLER

LAMENT FOR THE ALAMO

Davy Crockett in his woodman dress,
    His shirt of the hide of a yearling doe
And his coonskin cap and his rifle, Bess—
    Dead he lies in the Alamo.

Ned the Bee-hunter with the coal-black curls,
    Straight as a spear shaft, lithe as a bow,
With a song for the world and a laugh for the girls—
    Dead he lies in the Alamo.

Colonel Bowie of the twelve-inch blade,
    Gentle of speech and sure of blow,
Prone on the heap that his sword arm made—
    Dead he lies in the Alamo.

Stout were their hearts the red week long
  That they strove with the hordes of Mexico,
But their powder failed and the odds were strong—
  Dead they lie in the Alamo.

Back to back in the slaughter pen,
  Steel to the steel of a ruthless foe,
Travis fell with his nine-score men—
  Dead they lie in the Alamo.

Gone from the wood and the waterside,
  Gone from the haunts of the buffalo,
They ride no more where they loved to ride—
  Dead they lie in the Alamo.

Texans, plainsmen, pioneers,
  Pay the debt that your rifles owe:
Pay your debt of blood and tears
  For those who died in the Alamo!

ARTHUR GUITERMAN

THEY WILL LOOK FOR A FEW WORDS

The fast express for Gettysburg roared north
Among the hills one autumn day long gone,
At thirty miles an hour, from Washington
To the great Field; and beating along the ties,
Crying across the rivers, on it drew,
Echoing under bleak November skies.

The coaches rocked. One awkward traveler rode
Hunched in his seat, too tall for comfort there,
A gaunt, plain man with memorable air
Who talked at intervals with other men—
Companionable, keen of word—and then
Lapsed into silence, with his brooding look
Long on the changing scene, mile after mile—
A strange man, musing strangely, deeply, while
The rest talked on, or counted ties.

                    After a long, long time
Somebody reckoned the journey was half gone,
And all thoughts turned together to the town
Where soon the crowds would meet to praise their dead,
Their numberless dead, living in memory.

The tall man's eyes grew darker. "They will look
For a few words from me," slowly he said,
And, searching clumsily for paper, spread
A crumpled scrap across his dusty knee.

Then while the long train on and upward beat,
His pencil slowly stumbled through the grime
On the smudged sheet. And as the breathless climb
Conquered the longest rise of all, and topped
A hill above a plain far-flung and broad,
The pencil wrote, *This nation under God* . . .
Then, shaken through phrase by phrase, after a time
Wrote, *Shall not perish from the earth* . . . and stopped.

NANCY BYRD TURNER

SHILOH, A REQUIEM

Skimming lightly, wheeling still,
  The swallows fly low
Over the field in clouded days,
  The forest field of Shiloh—
Over the field where April rain
Solaced the parched one stretched in pain
Through the pause of night
That followed the Sunday fight
  Around the church of Shiloh—
The church so lone, the log-built one,
That echoed to many a parting groan
  And natural prayer
  Of dying foemen mingled there—
Foemen at morn, but friends at eve—
  Fame or country least their care:
(What like a bullet can undeceive!)
  But now they lie low,
While over them the swallows skim,
  And all is hushed at Shiloh.

HERMAN MELVILLE

ACHILLES DEATHERIDGE

"Your name is Achilles Deatheridge?
How old are you, my boy?"
"I'm sixteen past and I went to the war
From Athens, Illinois."

"Achilles Deatheridge, you have done
A deed of dreadful note."
"It comes of his wearing a battered hat,
And a rusty, wrinkled coat."

"Why, didn't you know how plain he is?
And didn't you ever hear,
He goes through the lines by day or night
Like a sooty cannoneer?

"You must have been half dead for sleep,
For the dawn was growing bright."
"Well, Captain, I had stood right there
Since six o'clock last night.

"I cocked my gun at the swish of the grass,
And how am I at fault
When a dangerous-looking man won't stop
When a sentry hollers halt?

"I cried out halt and he only smiled,
And waved his hand like that.
Why, any Johnnie could wear the coat,
And any fellow the hat.

"I hollered halt again and he stopped,
And lighted a fresh cigar.

I never noticed his shoulder badge,
And I never noticed a star."

"So you arrested him? Well, Achilles,
When you hear the swish of the grass,
If it's General Grant inspecting the lines
Hereafter let him pass."

EDGAR LEE MASTERS

THE AGED STRANGER

"I was with Grant," the stranger said.
    Said the farmer: "Say no more,
But rest thee here at my cottage porch,
    For thy feet are weary and sore."

"I was with Grant—" the stranger said.
    Said the farmer: "Nay, no more,—
I prithee sit at my frugal board,
    And eat of my humble store.

"How fares my boy,—my soldier boy,
    Of the old Ninth Army Corps?
I warrant he bore him gallantly
    In the smoke and the battle's roar!"

"I know him not," said the aged man,
    "And, as I remarked before,
I was with Grant—" "Nay, nay, I know,"
    Said the farmer, "Say no more.

"He fell in battle,—I see, alas!
    Thou'dst smooth these tidings o'er,—
Nay, speak the truth, whatever it be,
    Though it rend my bosom's core.

"How fell he?—with his face to the foe,
    Upholding the flag he bore?
Oh, say not that my boy disgraced
    The uniform that he wore!"

"I cannot tell," said the aged man,
    "And should have remarked before,
That I was with Grant—in Illinois—
    Some three years before the war."

Then the farmer spake him never a word,
    But beat with his fist full sore
That aged man, who had worked for Grant
    Some three years before the war.

BRET HARTE

ROBERT E. LEE
FROM *John Brown's Body*

And now at last,
Comes Traveller and his master. Look at them well.
The horse is an iron-grey, sixteen hands high,
Short back, deep chest, strong haunch, flat legs, small
     head,
Delicate ear, quick eye, black mane and tail,
Wise brain, obedient mouth.
              Such horses are
The jewels of the horseman's hands and thighs,
They go by the word and hardly need the rein.
They bred such horses in Virginia then,
Horses that were remembered after death
And buried not so far from Christian ground
That if their sleeping riders should arise
They could not witch them from the earth again
And ride a printless course along the grass
With the old manage and light ease of hand.
The rider now.
       He too, is iron-grey,
Though the thick hair and thick, blunt-pointed beard
Have frost in them.

    *   *   *   *   *

The man was loved, the man was idolized,
The man had every just and noble gift.
He took great burdens and he bore them well,
Believed in God but did not preach too much,
Believed and followed duty first and last
With marvellous consistency and force,
Was a great victor, in defeat as great,

No more, no less, always himself in both,
Could make men die for him but saved his men
Whenever he could save them—was most kind
But was not disobeyed—was a good father,
A loving husband, a considerate friend:
Had little humor, but enough to play
Mild jokes that never wounded, but had charm,
Did not seek intimates, yet drew men to him,
Did not seek fame, did not protest against it,
Knew his own value without pomp or jealousy
And died as he preferred to live—sans phrase,
With commonsense, tenacity and courage.

*   *   *   *   *

He was a man, and as a man he knew
Love, separation, sorrow, joy and death.
He was a master of the tricks of war,
He gave great strokes and warded strokes as great.
He was the prop and pillar of a State,
The incarnation of a national dream,
And when the State fell and the dream dissolved
He must have lived with bitterness itself—
But what his sorrow was and what his joy,
And how he felt in the expense of strength,
And how his heart contained its bitterness,
He will not tell us.

STEPHEN VINCENT BENÉT

NAMES FROM THE WAR

Once the land had no great names and no history.

It was a good land, with wood lots holding shadows beside the hot fields, blue hills hazy on the horizon, country roads going in aimless meanders from creek bottom and country store to places of no particular importance.

Nothing ever happened in it, except that men made homes and towns, with springtime plowing and autumn gathering,

Finding their drama in corn-huskings and barn-raisings, and in gay tin-pan chivarees for the young married couples,

Building churches by little groves, looking off the earth into mystery beyond mounded graves,

Wresting a living from the land, trying to get ahead, having a good life, happy because the world left them alone.

They put names on towns and crossroads and rivers, borrowing harsh words the Indians had left behind, using homespun words of their own, naming their land so they could know it.

The names had no ring or shine to them, then. They were just names, put there so that a man could say where he was.

A man could put in a crop beside Peachtree Creek, or hunt doves on the slope of Culp's Hill, or follow the clank of a cowbell into White Oak Swamp, or try for catfish in Stone's River—

There was nothing in any of those names to stir remembrance and grief, nothing to put a catch in the throat or send one's thoughts far into the mystery beyond the silent sky.
Not then.

Then the armies came and the names became terrible.
The armies tramped the lazy roads to ruin, raising endless dust clouds for a pillar of smoke by day,
Lighting thousands of campfires for a pillar of fire by night,
Tiny fires that glowed on lonely bivouacs just this side of nowhere.
By the campfires boys looked into the dark to the home places they might not see again
(Not looking ahead because of what they might see tomorrow),
Writing letters to the folks to say where they were.
And the postmarks on the letters carried the names, names that had grown menacing and evil,
Names that would echo in American life forever afterward, telling of fire on farm and hilltop, speaking of the thousands who found the end of the road in some obscure place they had never heard of.
The letters carried the commonplace news of the camp—
We had hardtack and salt pork again today. . . . Lots of the boys are sick. . . . I wish I could get some cold water from the spring behind our house at home. . . . Maybe we won't have a big fight for a day or two yet . . .
And sometimes the news from the battle front reached home before the letters did, so that what the writers said came from beyond the grave,

And the people back home looked at the postmarks, reading the names that meant fear and heartache and
undying loneliness.

Those strange country names from the war—
Sharpsburg and Spotsylvania, Pittsburg Landing and
Brices Cross Roads, Chickamauga and Gaines' Mill,
Milliken's Bend, Olustee, Bentonville, Gettysburg,
Corinth, Manassas, Cross Keys, Mechanicsville,
Chattanooga, Franklin, Resaca, Dover—
Quiet names of doom, stamped on soiled envelopes, going
across all of America, weaving a crimson thread into
the nation's memory, names that many families would
never dare say again—
Not until years and the growth of quiet pride had done
their work.

There were other names that did not get on the postmarks,
Names given to stray bits of landscape, grown equally
grim because death and anguish lay upon them—
Missionary Ridge, the Wilderness, Cemetery Ridge, Mal-
vern Hill, the West Wood and the East Wood, Snake
Creek Gap, Cedar Creek;
And the names that came straight from the battlefields,
coined by the men who fought,
Names like Bloody Lane and the Bloody Angle, the
Round Forest, Battery Wagner, the Peach Orchard,
the Sunken Road, Devil's Den, the Wheatfield and
the Cornfield;
Names of churches—Shiloh, New Hope, Dallas, and the
Dunker church;
Names of the houses people had lived in—Widow Tapp
and Widow Glenn, the Mumma House and the
Henry House, Chantilly;

Names like the Emmitsburg road and the Valley Pike,
and at last the haunted road that led past Sailor's
Creek to Appomattox;
Names that will live as long as America remembers.

The agony is gone, the grief and the loneliness are over,
with those who grieved going to join the men they
mourned;
The bitterness and the hot bewildered fury have faded out;
The last of the tragic overtones has echoed off to stillness
beyond the horizon.
But the names remain, never to be forgotten, never again
to be simple place names from a land history had
passed by.
What America was is in them;
What America is grew out of them;
What America finally will mean rings through them.
They still clang when we touch them. They are trans-
muted by what they say of America's greatest ex-
perience,
America's most profound and touching mystery.

BRUCE CATTON

ANNE RUTLEDGE

Out of me, unworthy and unknown,
The vibrations of deathless music;
"With malice toward none, with charity for all."
Out of me the forgiveness of millions toward millions,
And the beneficent face of a nation
Shining with justice and truth.
I am Anne Rutledge who sleep beneath these weeds,
Beloved in life of Abraham Lincoln,
Wedded to him, not through union,
But through separation.
Bloom forever, O Republic,
From the dust of my bosom!

EDGAR LEE MASTERS

ABRAHAM LINCOLN WALKS
AT MIDNIGHT

It is portentous, and a thing of state
That here at midnight, in our little town
A mourning figure walks, and will not rest,
Near the old courthouse pacing up and down,

Or by his homestead, or in shadowed yards
He lingers where his children used to play,
Or through the market, on the well-worn stones
He stalks until the dawn-stars burn away.

A bronzed, lank man! His suit of ancient black,
A famous high top-hat and plain worn shawl
Make him the quaint great figure that men love,
The prairie-lawyer, master of us all.

He cannot sleep upon his hillside now.
He is among us:—as in times before!
And we who toss and lie awake for long
Breathe deep, and start, to see him pass the door.

His head is bowed. He thinks on men and kings.
Yea, when the sick world cries, how can he sleep?
Too many peasants fight, they know not why,
Too many homesteads in black terror weep.

The sins of all the war-lords burn his heart.
He sees the dreadnaughts scouring every main.
He carries on his shawl-wrapped shoulders now
The bitterness, the folly, and the pain.

He cannot rest until a spirit-dawn
Shall come;—the shining hope of Europe free:
The league of sober folk, the Workers' Earth,
Bringing long peace to Cornland, Alp, and Sea.

VACHEL LINDSAY

PLATO TOLD HIM

plato told

him: he couldn't
believe it(jesus

told him; he
wouldn't believe
it)lao

tsze
certainly told
him,and general
(yes

mam)
sherman;
and even
(believe it
or

not)you
told him: i told
him;we told him
(he didn't believe it, no

sir)it took
a nipponized bit of
the old sixth

avenue
el;in the top of his head:to tell

him

E. E. CUMMINGS

SUNDAY: NEW GUINEA

The bugle sounds the measured call to prayers,
The band starts bravely with a clarion hymn,
From every side, singly, in groups, in pairs,
Each to his kind of service comes to worship Him.

Our faces washed, our hearts in the right place,
We kneel or stand or listen from our tents;
Half-naked natives with their kind of grace
Move down the road with balanced staffs like mendicants.

And over the hill the guns bang like a door
And planes repeat their mission in the heights.
The jungle outmaneuvers creeping war
And crawls within the circle of our sacred rites.

I long for our dishevelled Sundays home,
Breakfast, the comics, news of latest crimes,
Talk without reference, and palindromes,
Sleep and the Philharmonic and the ponderous *Times*.

I long for lounging in the afternoons
Of clean intelligent warmth, my brother's mind,
Books and thin plates and flowers and shining spoons,
And your love's presence, snowy, beautiful, and kind.

KARL SHAPIRO

ATLANTIC CHARTER, A.D. *1620–1942*

What are you carrying Pilgrims, Pilgrims?
What did you carry beyond the sea?
   We carried the Book, we carried the Sword,
   A steadfast heart in the fear of the Lord,
   And a living faith in His plighted word
   That all men should be free.

What were your memories, Pilgrims, Pilgrims?
What of the dreams you bore away?
   We carried the songs our fathers sung
   By the hearths of home when they were young,
   And the comely words of the mother-tongue
   In which they learnt to pray.

What did you find there, Pilgrims, Pilgrims?
What did you find beyond the waves?
   A stubborn land and a barren shore,
   Hunger and want and sickness sore:
   All these we found and gladly bore
   Rather than be slaves.

How did you fare there, Pilgrims, Pilgrims?
What did you build in that stubborn land?

We felled the forest and tilled the sod
Of a continent no man had trod
And we established there, in the Grace of God,
The rights whereby we stand.

What are you bringing us, Pilgrims, Pilgrims?
Bringing us back in this bitter day?
    The selfsame things we carried away:
    The Book, the Sword,
    The fear of the Lord,
    And the boons our fathers dearly bought:
    Freedom of Worship, Speech and Thought,
    Freedom from Want, Freedom from Fear,
    The liberties we hold most dear,
    And who shall say us Nay?

FRANCIS BRETT YOUNG

KOREA BOUND, 1952

Braced against the rise and fall of ocean,
holding the rail, we listen to the shrill
complaining of the waves against the hull,
and see the Golden Gate rise with our motion.
Some hours previous, bearing duffels
as heavy as our thoughts, we wound inward
like slaves in some gigantic pyramid,
selected by our Pharaoh for burial
against our wills. Now we watch Alcatraz
sink into the water, and visualize
the pale, amorphous masks of prisoners,
whose lack of freedom guarantees their lives.

WILLIAM CHILDRESS

IN A BAR NEAR
SHIBUYA STATION, TOKYO

The Japanese next to me at the bar
bites at his saké with big irregular teeth.
Behind the heavy glasses (which he wears
like an elegant suit of clothes) his eyes
are yellow as the warm wine he is drinking.

He turns like a door opening and says
with an aggressive softness, "USA?"

I nod, waiting to see the color of his mind.

"I was wounded at Okinawa."
The words drop reluctantly from his mouth
like drops of wine from the bottom of the bottle.

I set my weight on the soles of my feet
and keep a careful eye on his hands.
He pulls up his sleeve. The scar cries out
along his arm like an exclamation mark.
What words do you speak to an accusing wound?
He looks at the scar as a man looks at a bug
crawling his skin, with interest and loathing,
wishing that it would simply go away.

"I'm sorry," I say. The words in their silly weakness
vibrate in the vivid lamplight of the bar
before they fall to the floor with a shamed rustle.

He clenches and unclenches his fist. The scar ripples.

I lift my hands. I am ready, like a new kid
uneasy on a school ground the first day.

"American doctor fix my arm good," he says.
And then his face collapses into a smile.
"He not fix good, I not pick up saké now."

He lifts the blue-glazed, lovely curving cup
and gestures gently toward me. Shyly his eyes
move over mine like a friendly hand. We drink.

He puts the cup down carefully on the bar
with a brave lightness, as if it were a bomb
waiting to go off and blast his hand.

His face goes back to being merely a face.

Outside, Tokyo growls like a hunting tiger.

PAUL ENGLE

ON A CERTAIN ENGAGEMENT
SOUTH OF SEOUL

A long time, many years, we've had these wars.
When they were opened, one can scarcely say.
We were high school students, no more than sophomores,

When Italy broke her peace on a dark day,
And that was not the beginning. The following years
Grew crowded with destruction and dismay.

When I was nineteen, once the surprising tears
Stood in my eyes and stung me, for I saw
A soldier in a newsreel clutch his ears

To hold his face together. Those that paw
The public's bones to eat the public's heart
Said far too much, of course. The sight, so raw

And unbelievable, of people blown apart
Was enough to numb us without that bark and whine.
We grew disconsolate. Each had his chart

To mark on the kitchen wall the battle-line,
But many were out of date. The radio
Droned through the years, a faithful anodyne.

Yet the news of this slight encounter somewhere below
Seoul stirs my remembrance: we were a few,
Sprawled on the stiff grass of a small plateau,

Afraid. No one was dead. But we were new—
We did not know that probably none would die.
Slowly, then, all vision went askew.

My clothing was outlandish; earth and sky
Were metallic and horrible. We were unreal,
Strange bodies and alien minds; we could not cry

For even our eyes seemed to be made of steel;
Nor could we look at one another, for each
Was a sign of fear, and we could not conceal

Our hatred for our friends. There was no speech.
We sat alone, all of us, trying to wake
Some memory of the selves beyond our reach.

That place was conquered. The nations undertake
Another campaign now, in another land,
A stranger land perhaps. And we forsake

The miseries there that we can't understand
Just as we always have. And yet my glimpse
Of a scene on the distant field can make my hand

Tremble again. How quiet we are. One limps.
One cannot walk at all. Or one is all right.
But one owns this experience that crimps

Forgetfulness, especially at night.
Is this a bond? Does this make us brothers?
Or does it bring our hatred back? I might

Have known, but now I do not know. Others
May know. I know when I walk out-of-doors
I have a sorrow not wholly mine, but another's.

HAYDEN CARRUTH

BACK AGAIN FROM YUCCA FLATS

I saw it light the cactus sky
And all the physicists were there,
Galileo, Gauss and Boyle,
Electric currents in their hair:

Roger Bacon, Mariotte,
Volta, Ohm, and Faraday,
And four and twenty blackbirds
They screamed and flew away:

Eve and Eve Curie,
And David with his functional sling:
He would have searched in vain for pebbles
Across that fused Goliath's ring.

REEVE SPENCER KELLEY

TRACTION: NOVEMBER 22, 1963

His brother said that pain was what he knew.
Pain's wit is irony. It took two
Bullets to bring that straight back down. They said
One bullet had exploded in his head.

The unforeseen becomes inevitable.
Who would have thought, on that bloody day,
That back that had survived the terrible
Would take the head down with it all the way?

We saw another back. It killed the killer,
Who had killed twice. Three murders done,
The one before our eyes like a cheap thriller,
Run and re-run. That week-end of the gun,

Twenty-one salutes, his epitaph,
Back-fired on a billion screens at noon.
We loved his luck until it broke in half.
The end comes back. It always comes too soon.

HOWARD MOSS

CHANNEL U.S.A.—LIVE

We were all passengers in that motorcade,
caught in the dust of a far street
and the stars of flags blown, as the car moved,
bubble-top down, brown hair tossed
above a face familiar as our own.

At home in easy chairs, turning a dial
to bring the image close—the smile, the wave,
the harps of motorcycles and of cheers—
we were, in spite of miles or parties, there;
and ride there still, the underpass ahead,
a building's shadow falling like a tomb
across the narrowing street, the dust, this room
in California-Iowa-Maine,
            the rifle ready, aimed.

Most screens are black and white,
and blood seems only a darker stain.

The carpet's pastel color stays the same,
sofas unblotched. But one fabric turned red
where his torn head had lain.

He campaigned on crutches once;
once scratched a message on a savage coast,
swam more than once through pain,
rescued lost comrades, fought the foam
of inactivity in high, white beds,
worked toward action, wrote,
replaced a brother whom we never knew,
climbed up from foreign fields and died at home
in a loud street where a rifle leaned
its long, blue beak,
         ready and aimed.

A wreath lies where the bullet stopped.
A continent beyond, a live torch burns,
and we, by limousine and plane and jeep,
ride in the flickering caravan,
still caught on an unsteady screen
where westerns blast and haunt our sleep,
making each day the long commute
out of the muck of every street
toward a reviving flame.

We all were passengers, and are,
driving and driven through the sweep
of shadows, sunlight, flags, and love—
but one of us stood up and faced
         the rifle that is always aimed,
and left the image that we keep.

ADRIEN STOUTENBURG

MEN

Our history is grave noble and tragic
We trusted the look of the sun on the green leaves
We built our towns of stone with enduring ornaments
We worked the hard flint for basins of water

We believed in the feel of the earth under us
We planted corn grapes apple-trees rhubarb
Nevertheless we knew others had died
Everything we have done has been faithful and dangerous

We believed in the promises made by the brows of women
We begot children at night in the warm wool
We comforted those who wept in fear on our shoulders
Those who comforted us had themselves vanished

We fought at the dikes in the bright sun for the pride of it
We beat drums and marched with music and laughter
We were drunk and lay with our fine dreams in the straw
We saw the stars through the hair of lewd women

Our history is grave noble and tragic
Many of us have died and are not remembered
Many cities are gone and their channels broken
We have lived a long time in this land and with honor.

ARCHIBALD MAC LEISH

Lonesome Water

But I never been way from here,
Never got going;
I've drunk lonesome water.
I'm bound to the hills.

—ROY HELTON

WESTERN MAGIC

There are no fairy-folk in our Southwest,
The cactus spines would tear their filmy wings,
There's no dew anywhere for them to drink
And no green grass to make them fairy rings.

But sometimes in a windless blur of dust
The impish twins of War and Chance go by,
Or after storms the Spider Woman mends
With thin drawn cloud, torn edges of the sky.

And there is one who plays upon the flute
In deep rock crevices where springs are found,—
'Twas at To-yallanne they saw him first,—
In April youths are magicked by the sound.

How dawns the turquoise horse, Johano-ai,
Races the sun in dust of glittering grains,
Or round Pelado Peak the Rainbow Boy
Goes dancing with the many-footed rains.

There are no fairy-folk in our Southwest,
But there are hours when prairie-dog and snake,
Black beetle and the tecolote owl
Between two winks their ancient forms will take,

Clad in white skins with shell shield glittering,
The sun, their chief, the Ancient road will walk,
Half in her sleep the mothering earth
Of older things than fairy-folk will talk.

MARY AUSTIN

LONESOME WATER

Drank lonesome water:
Weren't but a tad then
Up in a laurel thick
Digging for sang;
Came on a place where
The stones was holler;
Something below them
Tinkled and rang.

Dug where I heard it
Dripping below me:
Should a knowed better,
Should a been wise;
Leant down and drank it,
Clutching and gripping
The overhung cliv
With the ferns in my eyes.

Tweren't no tame water
I knowed in a minute;
Must a been laying there
Projecting round
Since winter went home;
Must a laid like a cushion,
Where the feet of the blossoms
Was tucked in the ground.

Tasted of heart leaf,
And that smells the sweetest,
Paw paw and spice bush
And wild brier rose;

Must a been counting
The heels of the spruce pines,
And neighboring round
Where angelica grows.

I'd drunk lonesome water,
I knowed in a minute:
Never larnt nothing
From then till today;
Nothing worth larning
Nothing worth knowing.
I'm bound to the hills
And I can't get away.

Mean sort of dried up old
Groundhoggy feller,
Laying out cold here
Watching the sky;
Poor as a whipporwill
Bent like a grass blade;
Counting up stars
Till they count too high.

I know where the grey foxes
Uses up yander;
Know what'll cure ye
Of ptisic or chills,
But I never been way from here,
Never got going;
I've drunk lonesome water.
I'm bound to the hills.

ROY   HELTON

TUMBLING MUSTARD

Born in a fence-corner,
raised in a coulee,
wedded in Nebraska,
parted on the Sound:
They call me Tumbling Mustard, "Hey Tumbling
Mustard, what's your business, listen Buddy,
where are you bound?"

Monday in Omaha,
Tuesday in Dakota,
one day in Memphis,
three in Allentown:
Mud roads and stony roads, concrete and maca-
dam, she would never leave me if I would
settle down.

Columbine and larkspur,
peony and dahlia,
cornflower, mayflower,
each has its place:
I am the tumble-weed that rolls across the prairies,
winds at the back of it, mountains in its face.

Tumble-weed, tumble-weed,
riding his velocipede
east side, west side,
all around the moon:
Denver, San Francisco, Winnipeg, and Dallas,
may be if the gas holds out we'll get there soon.

MALCOLM COWLEY

HANGMAN'S TREE

Where the Canyon spreads on either hand
The Santiago Road is spanned
At one point by a famous tree,
A landmark in our history:
A sycamore, propped and old,
Of which a tingling tale is told
Of blood and wrath—the wild warped ways
Of wild warped men in former days.

When Flores made his desperate leap,
Man and horse, from the peak
That bears his name, two of his band
The vigilante caught and hanged
Upon this tree, summarily,
With savage grim celerity.
Long moldering in their graves they've lain,
The smoldering slayers and the slain.
But buried be their sins and lust?
Awaiting judgment with their dust?
The folk say, Nay; the violent keep
Not to the tomb, nor do they sleep.

When the pale moon rolls in rack of cloud,
And barely glints night's sullen shroud;
Or when her sickly yellow glow
Blurs through the fog-wisps rising slow
And swirling round the hills—ah, then
Return the restless souls of men.

Well may the wine-warmed straggler quake
At the ghostly sounds that upon him break:
The ring of hoof beats clattering near,
The scrape of boots, the clang of gear;
The whang and rasp of rope on bough,
The creak of limbs, the final sough;
And muffled shouts and oaths that pass—
A wan wind wailing down the grass.

And mortal eyes in terror see
Suspended from the fatal tree
And arching wide the road away,
Two phantom bandits swing and sway.

LILLIAN ZELLHOEFER WHITE

BETWEEN THE WALLS OF
THE VALLEY
Western Virginia, c. 1790

"I say, stranger,
The people up this hollow
Appear uncommon slim
To a traveler's eye.
Could you tell me why?"

*"The fat ones left for want of room
Between the walls of the valley."*

"Down there, stranger,
I saw a man lie moaning
In helpless misery

And about to die.
Could you tell me why?"

"Fell out of the field and broke his neck
Between the walls of the valley."

"You know, stranger,
Today I saw a wagon
With wheels on one side low
And one side high.
Could you tell me why?"

"To drive along the old bench road
Between the walls of the valley."

"It's odd, stranger,
I saw a farmer loading
His shotgun full of corn
As I went by.
Could you tell me why?"

"He shoots his corn in, row by row.
Between the walls of the valley."

"Last night, stranger,
At milking time a woman
Looked up her chimney tall
With her pail near by.
Could you tell me why?"

"To see if the cows were coming home
Between the walls of the valley."

"H'm! That *is* odd.

"I hear, stranger,
Your corn ears need no husking,
And they shell their own dry grains
When frost is high.
Could you tell me why?"

*"A strong wind blows them down the hill
Between the walls of the valley."*

"Hereabouts, stranger,
The cobbler pegs his soles on
But never sews the shoes
With a threaded eye.
Could you tell me why?"

*"Not room enough to pull his thread out
Between the walls of the valley."*

ELISABETH PECK

from THE PEOPLE, YES

They have yarns
Of a skyscraper so tall they had to put hinges
On the two top stories so to let the moon go by,
Of one corn crop in Missouri when the roots
Went so deep and drew off so much water
The Mississippi river bed that year was dry,
Of pancakes so thin they had only one side,
Of "a fog so thick we shingled the barn and six feet out
on the fog,"

Of Pecos Pete straddling a cyclone in Texas and riding it to the west coast where "it rained out under him,"

Of the man who drove a swarm of bees across the Rocky Mountains and the Desert "and didn't lose a bee,"

Of a mountain railroad curve where the engineer in his cab can touch the caboose and spit in the conductor's eye,

Of the boy who climbed a cornstalk growing so fast he would have starved to death if they hadn't shot biscuits up to him,

Of the old man's whiskers: "When the wind was with him his whiskers arrived a day before he did,"

Of the hen laying a square egg and cackling, "Ouch!" and of hens laying eggs with the dates printed on them,

Of the ship captain's shadow: it froze to the deck one cold winter night,

Of mutineers on that same ship put to chipping rust with rubber hammers,

Of the sheep counter who was fast and accurate: "I just count their feet and divide by four,"

Of the man so tall he must climb a ladder to shave himself,

Of the runt so teeny-weeny it takes two men and a boy to see him,

Of mosquitoes: one can kill a dog, two of them a man,

Of a cyclone that sucked cookstoves out of the kitchen, up the chimney flue, and on to the next town,

Of the same cyclone picking up wagon-tracks in Nebraska and dropping them over in the Dakotas,

Of the hook-and-eye snake unlocking itself into forty pieces, each piece two inches long, then in nine seconds flat snapping itself together again,

Of the watch swallowed by the cow—when they butchered
    her a year later the watch was running and had the
    correct time,

Of horned snakes, hoop snakes that roll themselves where
    they want to go, and rattlesnakes carrying bells in-
    stead of rattles on their tails,

Of the herd of cattle in California getting lost in a giant
    redwood tree that had hollowed out,

Of the man who killed a snake by putting its tail in its
    mouth so it swallowed itself,

Of railroad trains whizzing along so fast they reach the
    station before the whistle,

Of pigs so thin the farmer had to tie knots in their tails
    to keep them from crawling through the cracks in
    their pens,

Of Paul Bunyan's big blue ox, Babe, measuring between
    the eyes forty-two ax-handles and a plug of Star to-
    bacco exactly,

Of John Henry's hammer and the curve of its swing and
    his singing of it as "a rainbow round my shoulder."

    "Do tell!"
    "I want to know!"

CARL SANDBURG

STRAWS

Have you no weathervane?
   Then try the pond.
Is still water this side
   Of the isle, or beyond?

Or look at the chimney:
   The smoke-wreath will show
Better than iron
   Which way the winds blow.

Weathervanes sometimes
   Grow rusty, and fail,
But a horse will stand *always*
   Backed up to a gale.

ELIZABETH COATSWORTH

MOUNTAIN MEDICINE

To mend their every hurt, to heal all their ills,
The forest-wise folk of our green Southern hills
Turn to old pharmacopoeias, open wide
On the tip-tilted shelves of each mountainside.

To ginseng and mullein and shonny-haw bark,
To daffy-down dilly and to Noah's ark,
To boneset, spikenard and robin-runs-away,
To hackmatack, hurr-burr and Queen-for-a-day.

To ease their every ache, to lessen each pain,
Our woods-taught hill folk turn time and time again
To mountain panaceas, green cure-alls which grow
But seldom, or never, in valleys below.

To maypop, mistletoe, wild cherry and white pine,
To star-grass, sassafras and strawberry vine,
To elder flowers, balsam buds, catnip, too,
To simpler's joy and true-love and shoo-fly, shoo!

ELIZABETH-ELLEN LONG

NEGRO SPIRITUALS

We do not know who made them.
The lips that gave them birth
Are dust in the slaves' burying ground,
Anonymous as earth.

The poets, the musicians,
Were bondsmen bred and born.
They picked the master's cotton,
They hoed the master's corn.

The load was heavy on their backs,
The way was long and cold,
—But out of stolen Africa,
The singing river rolled,
And David's hands were dusky hands,
But David's harp was gold.

ROSEMARY and STEPHEN VINCENT BENÉT

SWING LOW, SWEET CHARIOT

I looked over Jordan, and what did I see
    Coming for to carry me home?
A band of angels coming after me,
    Coming for to carry me home.

Oh, if you get there before I do,
    Coming for to carry me home,
Tell all my friends I'm coming too,
    Coming for to carry me home.

Swing low, Sweet Chariot,
Coming for to carry me home.
Swing low, Sweet Chariot,
Coming for to carry me home.

AUTHOR UNKNOWN

JESSE JAMES

Jesse James was a man, and he had a robber band;
And he flagged down the eastern bound train.
Robert Ford watched his eye,
And he shot him on the sly,
And they laid Jesse James in his grave.

Poor old Jesse, poor old Jesse James,
And they laid Jesse James in his grave.
Robert Ford's pistol ball,
Brought him tumbling from the wall,
And they laid Jesse James in his grave.

Jesse James' little wife
Was a moaner all her life,
When they laid Jesse James in his grave.
She earned her daily bread
By her needle and her thread,
When they laid Jesse James in his grave.

AUTHOR UNKNOWN

CUMBERLAND GAP

Cumberland Gap is a noted place,
Cumberland Gap is a noted place,
Cumberland Gap is a noted place;
Three kinds of water for to wash your face.

Cumberland Gap with its cliff and rocks,
Cumberland Gap with its cliff and rocks,
Cumberland Gap with its cliff and rocks;
Home of the panther, and the bear and fox.

Daniel Boone stood on Pinnacle Rock,
Daniel Boone stood on Pinnacle Rock,
Daniel Boone stood on Pinnacle Rock;
He killed Indians with an old flintlock.

Lie down, boys, and take a little nap,
Lie down, boys, and take a little nap,
Lie down, boys, and take a little nap;
Fourteen miles to the Cumberland Gap.

AUTHOR UNKNOWN

BUFFALO BILL'S DEFUNCT

Buffalo Bill's
defunct
       who used to
       ride a watersmooth-silver
              stallion
and break onetwothreefourfive pigeonsjustlikethat
                         Jesus
he was a handsome man
            and what i want to know is
how do you like your blueeyed boy
Mister Death

E. E. CUMMINGS

JOHN HENRY

When John Henry was about three days old,
  A-sittin' on his pappy's knee,
He gave-a one long loud and-a lonesome cry,
  Said, 'Dat hammer'll be the death of me.'

Now John Henry said to his Captain one day,
  'A man ain't nothing but a man,
But before I'll be governed by an ole steam drill
  I'll die with my hammer in my hand.'

Now John Henry swung his hammer around of his head,
  And brought his hammer down on the ground.
A man in Chattanooga, two hundred miles away,
  Heard an awful rumbling sound.

Now John Henry had a pretty little gal,
   Her name was Polly Anne.
When John Henry was sick and a-layin' on his bed,
   Polly drove steel like a man.

When John Henry died, they wasn't no box
   Big enough to hold his bones,
So they buried him in a box-car deep in the ground,
   And let two mountains be his grave-stones.

AUTHOR UNKNOWN
Adapted by John Jacob Niles

A LEGEND OF PAUL BUNYAN

He came,
striding
over the mountain,
the moon slung on his back,
like a pack,
a great pine
stuck on his shoulder
swayed as he walked,
as he talked
to his blue ox
Babe;
a huge, looming shadow
of a man,
clad
in a mackinaw coat,
his logger's shirt
open at the throat
and the great mane of hair

matching
meeting
the locks of night,
the smoke from his cauldron pipe
a cloud on the moon
and his laugh
rolled through the mountains
like thunder
on a summer night
while the lightning of his smile
split the heavens
asunder.
His blue ox, Babe,
pawed the ground
till the earth
trembled
and shook
and a high cliff
toppled and fell:
and Babe's bellow
was fellow
to the echo
of Bunyan's laughter;
and then
with one step
he was in the next valley
dragging the moon after,
the stars
tangled,
spangled
in the branches of the great pine.
And as he left,
he whistled in the dark
like a far off train

blowing for a crossing
and plainly heard
were the plodding grunts
of Babe, the blue ox,
trying
to keep pace
from hill to hill,
and then, the sounds
fading,
dying,
were lost
in the churn of night,—
and all was still.

ARTHUR S. BOURINOT

DANIEL WEBSTER'S HORSES

If when the wind blows
Rattling the trees,
Clicking like skeletons'
Elbows and knees,

You hear along the road
Three horses pass—
Do not go near the dark
Cold window glass.

If when the first snow lies
Whiter than bones
You see the mark of hoofs
Cut to the stones,

Hoofs of three horses
Going abreast—
Turn about, turn about,
A closed door is best!

Upright in the earth
Under the sod
They buried three horses
Bridled and shod,

Daniel Webster's horses—
He said as he grew old,
"Flesh, I loved riding,
Shall I not love it, cold?

"Shall I not love to ride
Bone astride bone,
When the cold wind blows
And snow covers stone?

"Bury them on their feet
With bridle and bit.
They were fine horses—
See their shoes fit."

ELIZABETH COATSWORTH

THE APPLE-BARREL OF
JOHNNY APPLESEED

On the mountain peak, called "Going-To-The-Sun,"
I saw gray Johnny Appleseed at prayer
Just as the sunset made the old earth fair.
Then darkness came; in an instant, like great smoke,
The sun fell down as though its great hoops broke
And dark rich apples, poured from the dim flame
Where the sun set, came rolling toward the peak,
A storm of fruit, a mighty cider-reek,
The perfume of the orchards of the world,
From apple-shadows: red and russet domes
That turned to clouds of glory and strange homes
Above the mountain tops for cloud-born souls:—
Reproofs for men who build the world like moles,
Models for men, if they would build the world
As Johnny Appleseed would have it done—
Praying, and reading the books of Swedenborg
On the mountain top called "Going-To-The-Sun."

VACHEL LINDSAY

AMERICAN LAUGHTER

Oh, the men who laughed the American laughter
Whittled their jokes from the tough bull-pines;
They were tall men, sharpened before and after;
They studied the sky for the weather-signs;
They tilted their hats and they smoked long-nines!

Their laughter was ladled in Western flagons
And poured down throats that were parched for more;
This was the laughter of democrat wagons
And homely men at the crossroads store
—It tickled the shawl that a lawyer wore!

It hurt the ears of the dainty and pretty
But they laughed the louder and laughed their fill,
A laughter made for Virginia City,
Springfield, and Natchez-under-the-Hill,
And the river that flows past Hannibal still!

American laughter was lucky laughter,
A coonskin tune by a homespun bard;
It tasted of hams from the smokehouse rafter
And locust trees in the courthouse yard,
And Petroleum Nasby and Artemus Ward!

They laughed at the Mormons and Mike Fink's daughter,
And the corncob tale of Sut Lovingood's dog,
Till the ague fled from the fever-water
And the damps deserted the tree-stump bog,
—They laughed at the tale of the jumping frog!

They laughed at the British, they laughed at Shakers,
At Horace Greeley, and stovepipe hats;
They split their fences and ploughed their acres,
And treed their troubles like mountain-cats;
—They laughed calamity out of the flats!

Now the Boston man, according to rumor,
Said, as he turned in his high-backed bed,
"This doesn't conform to my rules for humor,"

And he settled his nightcap over his head,
—But it shook the earth like the buffalo-tread!

And the corn grew tall and the fields grew wider,
And the land grew sleek with the mirth they sowed;
They laughed the fat meat into the spider,
They laughed the blues from the Wilderness Road,
—They crossed hard times to the Comstock Lode!

KENNETH ALLAN ROBINSON

FOLK TUNE

When Bunyan swung his whopping axe
The forests strummed as one loud lute,
The timber crashed beside his foot
And sprung up stretching in his tracks.

He had an ox, but his was blue.
The flower in his buttonhole
Was brighter than a parasol.
He's gone. Tom Swift has vanished too,

Who worked at none but wit's expense,
Putting dirigibles together
Out in the yard, in the quiet weather,
Whistling behind Tom Sawyer's fence.

Now when the darkness in my street
Nibbles the last and crusty crumbs
Of sound, and all the city numbs
And goes to sleep upon its feet,

I listen hard to hear its dreams:
John Henry is our nightmare friend,
Whose shoulders roll without an end,
Whose veins pump, pump and burst their seams,

Whose sledge is smashing at the rock
And makes the sickly city toss
And half awake in sighs of loss
Until the screaming of the clock.

John Henry's hammer and his will
Are here and ringing out our wrong,
I hear him driving all night long
To beat the leisured snarling drill.

RICHARD WILBUR

The American Dimension:
Change and Diversity

Change and diversity are the meaning of our world: the American dimension. It is because the season changes, the weather changes, the country changes that the map goes on and on.

—ARCHIBALD MAC LEISH

COVERED BRIDGE

Bridges are essential in a place
Where hills tip up and mountain torrents race
Along each leaning farm and stonewall's shade.
Where snow comes deep, the bridges must be made
Like other houses, with a roof and eaves.
So a man's at home still though he leaves
His farm to cross the thunder of white waters
To visit with his neighbor's sons and daughters.
Trust New Englanders to make the useful good
And handsomeness out of the common wood.
Bridges which join the steep hills and white birches
Are made as carefully as are the churches;
A man goes over to his Monday duty
On a Sunday archway built of beauty:
His horse goes with loud feet through a neat room;
He sees a world of snow or summer's bloom
Ahead of him down at the narrow door,
But he is still house-bound and on a floor,
For all the heat or cold and smell of leather,
He is snug and out of all the weather.

ROBERT P. TRISTRAM COFFIN

MENDING WALL

Something there is that doesn't love a wall,
That sends the frozen-ground-swell under it,
And spills the upper boulders in the sun;
And makes gaps even two can pass abreast.

The work of hunters is another thing:
I have come after them and made repair
Where they have left not one stone on a stone,
But they would have the rabbit out of hiding,
To please the yelping dogs. The gaps I mean,
No one has seen them made or heard them made,
But at spring mending-time we find them there.
I let my neighbor know beyond the hill;
And on a day we meet to walk the line
And set the wall between us once again.
We keep the wall between us as we go.
To each the boulders that have fallen to each.
And some are loaves and some so nearly balls
We have to use a spell to make them balance:
"Stay where you are until our backs are turned!"
We wear our fingers rough with handling them.
Oh, just another kind of out-door game,
One on a side. It comes to little more:
There where it is we do not need the wall:
He is all pine and I am apple orchard.
My apple trees will never get across
And eat the cones under his pines, I tell him.
He only says, "Good fences make good neighbors."
Spring is the mischief in me, and I wonder
If I could put a notion in his head:
"*Why* do they make good neighbors? Isn't it
Where there are cows? But here there are no cows.
Before I built a wall I'd ask to know
What I was walling in or walling out,
And to whom I was like to give offence.
Something there is that doesn't love a wall,
That wants it down." I could say "Elves" to him,
But it's not elves exactly, and I'd rather
He said it for himself. I see him there

Bringing a stone grasped firmly by the top
In each hand, like an old-stone savage armed.
He moves in darkness as it seems to me,
Not of woods only and the shade of trees.
He will not go behind his father's saying,
And he likes having thought of it so well
He says again, "Good fences make good neighbors."

ROBERT FROST

GRAVEYARD

In the small New England places
Half the citizens have faces
Of marble or enduring granite.
Whatever the living do they scan it
From their hilltop on the sky.
When their good time came to die,
They did not creep away to be
Only a brief thin memory;
They took the center of the village
Where they could watch the toil and tillage
And see that all folks toe the mark
Between the morning star and dark.
We do our A B C's and pies
Better because those stony eyes
Of our old ones watch above us,
Because our marble fathers love us
And take pride in us from their graves.
Small wonder the smallest boy behaves!

ROBERT P. TRISTRAM COFFIN

MAINE

When old cars get retired, they go to Maine.
Thick as cows in backlots off the blacktop,
East of Bucksport, down the washboard
from Penobscot to Castine,
they graze behind frame barns: a Ford
turned tractor, Hudsons chopped to half-ton
trucks, and Chevvy panels, jacked up,
tireless, geared to saw a cord of wood.

Old engines never die. Not in Maine,
where men grind valves the way their wives grind axes.
Ring-jobs burned out down the Turnpike
still make revolutions, turned marine.
If Hardscrabble Hill makes her knock,
Maine rigs the water-jacket salt: a man
can fish forever on converted sixes,
and for his mooring, sink a V-8 block.

When fishing's poor, a man traps what he can.
When salt-rust speeds a Bangor hearse towards
death, the body still survives:
painted lobster, baited—off Route 1—
with home-preserves and Indian knives,
she'll net a parlor-full of Fords, and haul in
transient Cadillacs like crabs; Maine trades
in staying power, not shiftless drives.

PHILIP BOOTH

SQUARE-TOED PRINCES

My ancestors were fine, long men,
    Their hands were like square sails,
They ran the lengths of longitudes,
    Harpooning spouting whales.

Men to put a twinkle in
    The proud eyes of their Maker,
Standing up against the winds
    On the square toes of a Quaker.

From Baffin's Bay and Davis Strait
    To the Serpent of the South,
They had the whale-gaff in the fist
    And Scripture in the mouth.

Fingers like belaying pins,
    A heart like an ironed bucket,
Humble servants of the Lord,
    Princes of Nantucket.

The wallowing mammoths of the sea
    Felt their ruddy will
And quaked along the Torrid Line
    From Gold Coast to Brazil.

In notches on the mizzen-mast
    These men kept the tally;
Their hearts were the Rose of Sharon
    And the Lily of the Valley.

The Yankee grit was in their spines,
    Their voices were like guns;
They yearned to breed a nation up,
    They manned their ships with sons.

They brought home ambergris and oil
    In hogsheads and in tierces
And knelt down on their pineboard floors
    To thank God for his mercies.

Square-riggers were their trundle-beds,
    And they found their graves
In the sea or nigh the sea,
    Within the sound of waves.

They wrapped the ocean like a cloak
    And the shifting dunes above them;
They lie in peace till the Judgment Day
    When the Lord will rise and love them.

ROBERT P. TRISTRAM COFFIN

MY FATHERS CAME FROM KENTUCKY

I was born in Illinois—
Have lived there many days,
And I have Northern words,
And thoughts,
And ways.

But my great-grandfathers came
To the west with Daniel Boone,
And taught his babes to read,
And heard the redbird's tune;

And heard the turkey's call,
And stilled the panther's cry,
And rolled on the blue-grass hills,
And looked God in the eye.

And feud and Hell were theirs;
Love, like the moon's desire,
Love like a burning-mine,
Love like rifle-fire.

I tell tales out of school
Till these Yankees hate my style,
Why should the young lad cry,
Shout with joy for a mile?

Why do I faint with love
Till the prairies dip and reel?
My heart is a kicking horse
Shod with Kentucky steel.

No drop of my blood from north
Of Mason and Dixon's line.
And this racer in my breast
Tears my ribs for a sign.

But I ran in Kentucky hills
Last week. They were hearth and home . . .
Under the redbird's wings
Was peace and honeycomb.

VACHEL LINDSAY

HILL PEOPLE

They are not given much to laughter,
   These people, stanch as rock-ribbed hills,
And quietude increases after
   The stealthy snow drifts down and spills
On rugged slopes. Here strong men meet
   Around warm hearths, and their sparse speech,
Elizabethan, yet complete,
   Cracks like a rifle in the breach
Of silence. Fearless as the eagle,
   Their wants are whittled to the bone,
Yet born to freedom, they are regal
   And obdurate as stone.

HARRIET GRAY BLACKWELL

UNCLE AMBROSE

Your hair is growing long, Uncle Ambrose,
And the strands of your beard are like willow sprays
Hanging over Troublesome Creek's breeze in August.
Uncle Ambrose, your hands are heavy with years,
Seamy with the ax's heft, the plow's hewn stock,
The thorn wound and the stump-dark bruise of time.

Your face is a map of Knott County
With hard ridges of flesh, the wrinkled creek beds,
The traces and forks carved like wagon tracks on stone;
And there is Troublesome's valley struck violently
By a barlow's blade, and the anti-cline of all waters
This side of the Kentucky River.

Your teeth are dark-stained apples on an ancient tree
And your eyes the trout pools between the narrow hills;
Your hands are glacial drifts of stone
Cradled on a mountain top:
One is Big Ball Mountain, rock-ribbed and firm,
One the Appalachian range from Maine to Alabama.

JAMES STILL

KIVERS

Yes, I've sev'ral kivers you can see;
'Light and hitch your beastie in the shade!
I don't foller weaving now so free,
And all my purtiest ones my forebears made.
Home-dyed colors kindly meller down
Better than these new fotched-on ones from town.

I ricollect my granny at the loom
Weaving that blue one yonder on the bed.
She put the shuttle by and laid in tomb.
Her word was I could claim hit when I wed.
"Flower of Edinboro" was hits name,
Betokening the land from which she came.

Nary a daughter have I for the boon,
But there's my son's wife from the level land,
She took the night with us at harvest-moon—
A comely, fair young maid, with loving hand.
I gave her three—"Sunrise" and "Trailing Vine"
And "Young Man's Fancy." She admired 'em fine.

That green one mostly wrops around the bread;
"Tennessee Lace" I take to ride behind.
Hither and yon right smart of them have fled.
Inside the chest I keep my choicest kind—
"Pine-Bloom" and "St. Ann's Robe" (of hickory brown),
"Star of the East" (that yaller's fading down).

The Rose? I wove hit courting, long ago—
Not Simon, though he's proper kind of heart—
His name was Hugh—the fever laid him low—
I allus keep that kiver set apart.
"Rose of the Valley," he would laugh and say
"The kiver's favoring your face to-day!"

ANN COBB

APPALACHIAN FRONT

Panther lies next to Wharncliffe
and Wharncliffe next to Devon
and Devon next to Delorme.
In each a single fisherman casts
in the slow, black water of the Big Sandy.
Catfish is the whisker lurking
behind the bobbing cork.
He lives, it seems, in dense night
from day to day until the fisherman
from Wharncliffe pulls him out
to be fried in tin-roof, tarpaper shacks
from there to Matewan.

Politicians call this valley
a depressed area.
But, under the sun, my heart
will not have it so.
Straight up from the brackish water,
up the mountainside, green pointed trees
as close as bird's wings
grow fierce and clean,
and then for miles beside the tracks
the river moves faster over the rocks
and the water isn't black at all—
only the silt underneath.
The water over the rocks
is running clear and cold and pure.

ROBERT LEWIS WEEKS

135

from ‛REPORT FROM THE CAROLINAS*

It's a debatable land. The winds are variable,
Especially winds of doctrine, though the one
Prevailing breeze is mild, we say, and southerly.
We have a good deal of sun,

And our peach trees bloom too early. The first light
   promise
Is lightly kept in a Carolina spring
(It blows both hot and cold). Yet by February
There is the flowering

Of yellow jasmine and sudden gold forsythia,
And mockingbirds; at night the threat of snow.
Northerners passing on their way to Florida
Say it's not Florida, though,

This in-between land. There's the coastal region,
For instance, next a calm sea. Yet too near
Are the dangerous shoals, outlying and inhospitable.
One cape is called Cape Fear.

There's the Piedmont, where I live—the plateau uprising
Between high Appalachians and the sea.
It would seem a temperate world. We take our siestas;
Our ways are leisurely;

And people tend to speak to one another,
Observing the civilities. Seldom heard
Is bitter rebel talk now, seldom "Damnyankee"—
At least not as one word.

And everyone is a Democrat, almost,
Though argumentative. Not a few incline
Toward oratory still, being Southern orators.
Our grapes are muscadine;

Our works are amiable. We grow camellias
In Charleston gardens; we raise azalea flowers.
Both the Carolina wren and Whistler's mother
Are specialties of ours.

We have quail in the yard, and dogwood in the wood-
    lands,
A skyful of buzzards, the wisteria trees,
Pines and magnolias. Also, we have, lately,
Certain uncertainties—

HELEN BEVINGTON

IN THE MARBLE QUARRY

Beginning to dangle beneath
The wind that blows from the undermined wood,
    I feel the great pulley grind,

The thread I cling to lengthen
And let me soaring and spinning down into marble,
    Hooked and weightlessly happy

Where the squared sun shines
Back equally from all four sides, out of stone
    And years of dazzling labor,

To land at last among men
Who cut with power saws a Parian whiteness
   And, chewing slow tobacco,

   Their eyebrows like frost,
Shunt house-sized blocks and lash them to cables
   And send them heavenward

   Into small-town banks,
Into the columns and statues of government buildings,
   But mostly graves.

   I mount my monument and rise
Slowly and spinningly from the white-gloved men
   Toward the hewn sky

   Out of the basement of light,
Sadly, lifted through time's blinding layers
   On perhaps my tombstone,

   In which the original shape
Michelangelo believed was in every rock upon earth
   Is heavily stirring,

   Surprised to be an angel,
To be waked in North Georgia by the ponderous play
   Of men with ten-ton blocks

   But no more surprised than I
To feel sadness fall off as though I myself
   Were rising from stone

Held by a thread in midair,
Badly cut, local-looking, and totally uninspired,
    Not a masterwork

    Or even worth seeing at all
But the spirit of this place just the same,
    Felt here as joy.

JAMES DICKEY

NOCTURNE: GEORGIA COAST

The shrimping boats are late today;
The dusk has caught them cold.
Swift darkness gathers up the sun,
And all the beckoning gold
That guides them safely into port
Is lost beneath the tide.
Now the lean moon swings overhead,
And Venus, salty-eyed.

They will be late an hour or more,
The fishermen, blaming dark's
Swift mischief or the stubborn sea,
But as their lanterns' sparks
Ride shoreward at the foam's white rim,
Until they reach the pier
I cannot say if their catch is shrimp,
Or fireflies burning clear.

DANIEL WHITEHEAD HICKY

BAPTISM

We drive this Sunday south into the country,
Where a white frame Gothic church stands at the levee.
The Negroes, dressed in black, glistening with the heat,
Come early, carrying lunches, and stay late
In the steaming little church where they sing together.

Across the levee at the old landing they still
Hold their baptisms. A live religion deals
In living symbols; so they prefer the river,
Their untamed font of darkness. I recall one evening
When the red sun broke through colonnades of cloud,

And the two tides met, brown and golden, of earth and
      air—
Light calm and pure, and that violence of water—
How they went down in white and moaning lamentation,
To the mud-brown flood and under, then broke up sing-
      ing,
Rolled on the earth, reborn out of death and nature.

Here at the Christian crossroad we note the cleavage
Between the enlightened few with their stoic wisdom,
And the hungry soul of the many whose new Mystery
Is the beat of this spiritual jazz, the loved return
Down to the brown river and wounded Thammuz' blood.

Through all the aseptic channels of the modern
This wild release is pouring; are we who listen,
As the brooding ground and single imploration
Breaks in waves of answer, group-homing passion,
We whites, who can only listen, are blurred with our tears.

CHARLES G. BELL

THE GAR

When I go home to the South the river lakes
Call me to fish again. We drive in the dark;
By dawn we are tied at the willows. The sailor's warning
Flutes the green depths with red. Soon rain is falling.
We sit in a steady drizzle as corks go down,

And bland white perch come slithering through the air.
And now I have hooked the fish I strangely admire,
Tremendous thing, old prehistoric gar,
With armor plate and alligator jaw,
Who steals the bait, sweeps off, and breaks the line.

The fishermen all hate this fossil sign
Of the swamp past we share. My father would stave
Their heads, or if they were small, crack the bills
In his hands, cursing them as the devil's spawn.
And once near here we found old Foster seining.

The big net filled with spoonbills, catfish, drum;
And in their midst an alligator gar
Twice the size of a man was plunging wild,
Ripping it all to shreds. They hauled to the shore,
And Foster stood, a shape of violence,

141

The revolver crashing in his lowered hand,
As he pumped the slugs into the dark wallowing form. . . .
Now all around us the water works with gar
That rise and belch, sweep oily tails. Demons
Of the South, you are strong; time is yours; you will
    endure.

CHARLES G. BELL

SOUTHERN MANSION

Poplars are standing there still as death
And ghosts of dead men
Meet their ladies walking
Two by two beneath the shade
And standing on the marble steps.

There is a sound of music echoing
Through the open door
And in the field there is
Another sound tinkling in the cotton:
Chains of bondmen dragging on the ground.

The years go back with an iron clank,
A hand is on the gate,
A dry leaf trembles on the wall.
Ghosts are walking.
They have broken roses down
And poplars stand there still as death.

ARNA BONTEMPS

IN LOUISIANA

The long, gray moss that softly swings
    In solemn grandeur from the trees,
    Like mournful funeral draperies,—
A brown-winged bird that never sings.

A shallow, stagnant, inland sea,
    Where rank swamp grasses wave, and where
    A deadliness lurks in the air,—
A sere leaf falling silently.

The death-like calm on every hand,
    That one might deem it sin to break,
    So pure, so perfect,—these things make
The mournful beauty of this land.

ALBERT BIGELOW PAINE

TEXAS

I went a-riding, a-riding,
Over a great long plain.
And the plain went a-sliding, a-sliding
Away from my bridle rein.

Fields of cotton, and fields of wheat,
Thunder-blue gentians by a wire fence,
Standing cypress, red and tense,
Holding its flower rigid like a gun,
Dressed for parade by the running wheat,

By the little bouncing cotton. Terribly sweet
The cardinals sing in the live-oak trees,
And the long plain breeze,
The prairie breeze,
Blows across from swell to swell
With a ginger smell.
Just ahead, where the road curves round,
A long-eared rabbit makes a bound
Into a wheat field, into a cotton field,
His track glitters after him and goes still again
Over to the left of my bridle rein.

But over to the right is a glare—glare—glare—
Of sharp glass windows.
A narrow square of brick jerks thickly up above the cotton
    plants.
A raucous mercantile thing flaring the sun from thirty-six
    windows,
Brazenly declaring itself to the lovely fields.
Tramcars run like worms about the feet of this thing,
The coffins of cotton bales feed it,
The threshed wheat is its golden blood.
But here it has no feet,
It has only the steep ironic grin of its thirty-six windows,
Only its basilisk eyes counting the fields,
Doing sums of how many buildings to a city, all day and
    all night.

Once they went a-riding, a-riding,
Over the great long plain.
Cowboys singing to their dogie steers,
Cowboys perched on forty-dollar saddles,
Riding to the North, six months to get there,
Six months to reach Wyoming.

"Hold up, paint horse, herd the little dogies,
Over the lone prairie."
Bones of dead steers,
Bones of cowboys,
Under the wheat, maybe.

The skyscraper sings another way,
A tune of steel, of wheels, of gold.
And the ginger breeze blows, blows all day
Tanged with flowers and mold.
And the Texas sky whirls down, whirls down,
Taking long looks at the fussy town.
An old sky and a long plain
Beyond, beyond, my bridle rein.

AMY LOWELL

THE SOUND OF MORNING IN NEW MEXICO

At six o'clock
The sound of the bells
Calls from a pale rectangle
On the gray mesa—chimes,
Insistent but slow,
Pausing for solemn response.

The sun is not yet up;
The animals are still crying
From the tufted sage
And the barren foothills

Where dawn is a wavering thread,
Pink and lemon.

Now, from here and there
Among the mud houses,
Comes the knock and whirl
Of worn motors—the worshippers
Moving out behind flickering
Headlights, silencing
The coyotes and the bells.

REEVE SPENCER KELLEY

THE GRASS ON THE MOUNTAIN

Oh, long long
The snow has possessed the mountains.

The deer have come down and the big-horn,
They have followed the Sun to the South
To feed on the mesquite pods and the bunch grass.
Loud are the thunder drums
In the tents of the mountains.
Oh, long, long
Have we eaten chia seeds
And dried deer's flesh of the summer killing.
We are wearied of our huts
And the smoky smell of our garments.

We are sick with desire of the sun
And the grass on the mountains.

MARY AUSTIN

RAIN IN THE SOUTHWEST

It's raining again in the Southwest—wet
On the flat roofs, dripping from the vigas—
On the cities and the pueblos.
Even now, the rain is soaking into the brown walls
At San Felipe and Santo Domingo, close
Against the place where Little Buffalo
Is learning to draw pictures
Of forgotten animals—rain, rain, rain,
Over the high mesa, gathering in metallic brooks,
And down the lush valleys,
Shining on the hides of squashes.
The chief gives thanks.
The farmer grins.
The caballeros dance their mamacitas
Round the dust of their adobes
High in the lost and lonely hills,
Where centuries of hawks have quit
The dripping sky and centuries of weeds
Lie soaked against the rounded earth—
Rain on the pink crags, dulled to red,
Rain on the yellow slopes, dulled to ochre.
And on the highways, tightrope-walking
Their glistening way from death to daring,
The turtle wonders, the snake hides.

Great Albuquerque, a monstrous squat bird,
Nests like a phoenix on the Rio Grande,
Waiting the moment of the huge sun
To renew itself in fire—
Rain, rain,
On the high pines, in the low junipers,
On the sweet, husklike, but anxious desert.
The cotton bows, the chili gleams,
The lumber towns lie dank as warping boards
As, over all this up-and-down
Of canyon grand and mountain lost,
The rain pours down, remembering
Its promises to all its plants
And all its animals that their grotesqueness
Need not be increased
By a more desperate adaptation.

REEVE SPENCER KELLEY

ARIZONA VILLAGE

Here, houses close their sleepy window eyes
    At ten o'clock. Yet on a rocky hill
Beneath a half-drawn shade, a light defies
    The desert night. Soon old Judge Whippoorwill
Pronounces sentence, and a hoot owl cries,
"Who-oo-oo? Who-oo-oo? Who-oo-oo?"
A young bird answers clearly, "You-o-you!"
    Then all is still

148

Until across the oven sands is heard
    A lean coyote complaining to the moon.
One final yelp. He sniffs the desert air;
    Jack rabbits scamper off across the dune.
When he pursues, they run to shelter where
    The cactus bleeds red flowers. A chaparral cock
Is routed from the nest of twigs that he
    Made soft with skins of rattlesnakes. A rock
Goes crashing downward. Cries and clamor cease.
The pack rats scurry home—and suddenly
Comes desert peace.

ROBERT STILES DAVIEAU

*V*ACATION

    One scene as I bow to pour her coffee:—

        Three Indians in the scouring drouth
        huddle at a grave scooped in the gravel,
        lean to the wind as our train goes by.
        Someone is gone.
        There is dust on everything in Nevada.

    I pour the cream.

WILLIAM STAFFORD

KANSAS BOY

This Kansas boy who never knew the sea,
Walks through the young corn rippling at his knee
As sailors walk; and, when the grain grows higher,
Watches the dark waves leap with greener fire
Than ever oceans hold. He follows ships,
Tasting the bitter spray upon his lips,
For in his blood upstirs the salty ghost
Of one who sailed a storm-bound British coast.
Across wide fields he hears the sea winds crying,
Shouts at the crows—and dreams of white gulls flying.

RUTH LECHLITNER

ONE HOME

Mine was a Midwest home—you can keep your world.
Plain black hats rode the thoughts that made our code.
We sang hymns in the house; the roof was near God.

The light bulb that hung in the pantry made a wan light,
but we could read by it the names of preserves—
outside, the buffalo grass, and the wind in the night.

A wildcat sprang at Grandpa on the Fourth of July
when he was cutting plum bushes for fuel,
before Indians pulled the West over the edge of the sky.

To anyone who looked at us we said, "My friend";
liking the cut of a thought, we could say "Hello."
(But plain black hats rode the thoughts that made our
    code.)

WILLIAM STAFFORD

THE FLOWER-FED BUFFALOES

The flower-fed buffaloes of the spring
In the days of long ago,
Ranged where the locomotives sing
And the prairie flowers lie low;
The tossing, blooming, perfumed grass
Is swept away by wheat,
Wheels and wheels and wheels spin by
In the spring that still is sweet.
But the flower-fed buffaloes of the spring
Left us long ago.
They gore no more, they bellow no more,
They trundle around the hills no more:—
With the Blackfeet lying low,
With the Pawnees lying low.

VACHEL LINDSAY

THE COWBOY'S LIFE

The bawl of a steer,
To a cowboy's ear,
Is music of sweetest strain;
And the yelping notes
Of the gray coyotes
To him are a glad refrain.

For a kingly crown
In the noisy town
His saddle he wouldn't change;
No life so free
As the life we see
Way out on the Yaso range.

The rapid beat
Of his broncho's feet
On the sod as he speeds along,
Keeps living time
To the ringing rhyme
Of his rollicking cowboy song.

The winds may blow
And the thunder growl
Or the breezes may safely moan;—
A cowboy's life
Is a royal life
His saddle his kingly throne.

AUTHOR UNKNOWN
Adapted by John A. and Alan Lomax

MOONLIGHT

My father hated moonlight
And pulled the curtains down
Each time the snows of moonlight
Came drifting on the town.

He was an old frontiersman,
And on their deadly raids,
Comanches rode by moonlight
In stealthy cavalcades;

And took the settlers' horses,
Or left a trail of red—
He came to love the darkness,
And hated the moon, he said.

BERTA HART NANCE

THE WINNING OF THE TV WEST

When twilight comes to Prairie Street
On every TV channel,
The kids watch men with blazing guns
In jeans and checkered flannel.
Partner, the West is wild tonight—
There's going to be a battle
Between the sheriff's posse and
The gang that stole the cattle.

On every screen on Prairie Street
The sheriff roars his order:
"We've got to head those hombres off
Before they reach the border."
Clippoty-clop and bangity-bang
The lead flies left and right.
Paradise Valley is freed again
Until tomorrow night.
And all the kids on Prairie Street
Over and under ten
Can safely go to dinner now . . .
The West is won again.

JOHN T. ALEXANDER

ÉTUDE GÉOGRAPHIQUE

Out West, they say, a man's a man; the legend still persists
That he is handy with a gun and careless with his fists.
The fact is, though, you may not hear a stronger word
    than "Gosh!"
From Saskatoon, Saskatchewan, to Walla Walla, Wash.

In western towns 'tis many years since it was last the rage
For men to earn their daily bread by holding up a stage,
Yet story writers still ascribe such wild and woolly bosh
To Saskatoon, Saskatchewan, to Walla Walla, Wash.

The gents who roam the West today are manicured and
    meek,
They shave their features daily and they bathe three times
    a week.

They tote the tame umbrella and they wear the mild
    galosh
From Saskatoon, Saskatchewan, to Walla Walla, Wash.

But though the West has frowned upon its old nefarious
    games,
It still embellishes the map with sweet, melodious names,
Which grow in lush profusion like the apple and the
    squash
From Saskatoon, Saskatchewan, to Walla Walla, Wash.

STODDARD KING

DAKOTA BADLANDS

Beneath its morning caul, this ravaged land
    With all its inmost secrets torn apart,
Lies wrenched and broken in a giant's hand
    And joins its silent questions to my heart.
Who met a savage adversary here?
    What mighty angel wrestled with his twin?
And was it here that Lucifer fell clear
    Down onto earth in payment for his sin?
Or did some comet tail of ages old
    Once flick among these crags its serpent hiss?
The sun, now up, turns all of it to gold
    And heals the land with one quick lover's kiss.

ELIZABETH LANDEWEER

AUGUST FROM MY DESK

It is hot today, dry enough for cutting grain,
and I am drifting back to North Dakota
where butterflies are all gone brown with wheat dust.

And where some boy,
red-faced, sweating, chafed,
too young to be dying this way
steers a laborious, self-propelled combine,
and dreams of cities, and blizzards—
and airplanes.

With the white silk scarf of his sleeve
he shines and shines his goggles,
he checks his meters, checks his flaps,
screams contact at his dreamless father,
and, engines roaring,
he pulls back the stick

and hurtles into the sun.

ROLAND FLINT

HIGH WHEAT COUNTRY

The earth lies here in giant folds and creases—
  Great ridges rise against the light-blue sky,
The crazy-quilt fields mark the slopes in far-flung pieces,
  And, in between, the runnel-traced valleys lie.
Over long rise after rise the straight road narrows.
  The men and the machines in the fields are moving
    toys,
Trailed by streamers of dust from the puny harrows.
  The meadow larks spring; they whistle like startled
    boys.
This wild high country is tamed—how long, who knows?
Still, the dust devils swirl, the old wind blows.

ELIJAH L. JACOBS

THE FISH COUNTER AT BONNEVILLE

Downstream they have killed the river and built a dam;
by that power they wire to here a light:
a turbine strides high poles to spit its flame
at this flume going down. A spot glows white
where an old man looks on at the ghosts of the game
in the flickering twilight—deep dumb shapes that glide.
So many Chinook souls, so many Silverside.

WILLIAM STAFFORD

157

THE PIONEER WOMAN—IN THE NORTH COUNTRY

The eyes of the pioneer woman are blue, blue as the
  queen's velvet, clear as the skyey robes of Fra
  Angelico's angels.
There are no shadows in them.

Around us the country stretches, mile on mile, county on
  county, of wild unbroken ground.
Lakes are here, wide grey lakes that lie empty under the
  colorless sun of the north; and little familiar lakes,
  nestling among the trees.
Forests are here, scraggy, unkempt woods, too often
  lumbered, of jack-pine, scrub-oak and soft maple,
  choked with underbrush.
Wandering rutted roads are here, and untidy fences,
  shacks too quickly thrown together, and fields half-
  tilled.
At night the sun goes down in blood, loons cry across
  the lakes and far away the coyotes howl.
A strange land, a land half finished!

The forty acres of the pioneer are fifteen miles from town.
  Five miles away his nearest neighbor lives.
Yet the eyes of his wife are clear and unshadowed as
  emeralds in the sun.

"There are no blueberries this year or not enough to
  count," she says.
"I only put up forty quarts . . ."

EUNICE TIETJENS

MONTANA WIVES

I had to laugh,
For when she said it we were sitting by the door,
And straight down was the Fork
Twisting and turning and gleaming in the sun.
And then your eyes carried across the purple bench
    beyond the river
With the Beartooth Mountains fairly screaming with
    light and blue and snow
And fold and turn of rimrock and prairie as far as your
    eye could go.

And she says: "Dear Laura, sometimes I feel so sorry for
    you,
Shut away from everything—eating out your heart with
    loneliness.
When I think of my own full life I wish that I could
    share it.
Just pray for happier days to come, and bear it."

She goes back to Billings to her white stucco house,
And looks through net curtains at another white stucco
    house,
And a brick house,
And a yellow frame house,
And six trimmed poplar trees,
And little squares of shaved grass.

Oh, dear, she stared at me like I was daft.
I couldn't help it! I just laughed and laughed.

GWENDOLEN HASTE

SNOW COUNTRY

only
a little
yellow

school bus
creeping along
a thin

ribbon
of snow road
splashed color

on the white
winter canvas
that was

Wyoming
from the train
yesterday

DAVE ETTER

THE SHEEPHERDER

Loping along on the day's patrol,
I came on a herder in Jackson's Hole;
Furtive of manner, blazing of eye,
He never looked up when I rode by;
But counting his fingers, fiercely intent,
Around and around his herd he went:

> *One sheep, two sheep, three sheep, four . . .*
> *Twenty and thirty . . . forty more;*
> *Strayed—nine ewes; killed—ten rams;*
> *Seven and seventy lost little lambs.*

He was the only soul I could see
On the lonely range for company—
Save one lean wolf and a prairie-dog,

And a myriad of ants at the foot of a log;
So I sat the herder down on a clod—
But his eyes went counting the ants in the sod:

One sheep, two sheep, three sheep, four . . .
Fifty and sixty . . . seventy more;
There's not in this flock a good bell-wether!
Then how can a herder hold it together!

Seeking to cheer him in his plight,
I flung my blankets down for the night;
But he wouldn't talk as we sat by the fire—
Corralling sheep was his sole desire;
With fingers that pointed near and far,
Mumbling, he herded star by star:

One sheep, two sheep, three—as before!
Eighty and ninety . . . a thousand more!
My lost little lambs—one thousand seven!—
Are wandering over the hills of Heaven.

LEW SARETT

IN THE OREGON COUNTRY

From old Fort Walla Walla and the Klickitats
to Umpqua near Port Orford, stinking fish tribes
massacred our founders, the thieving Whites.

Chief Rotten Belly slew them at a feast;
Kamiakin riled the Snakes and Yakimas;
all spurted arrows through the Cascades west.

Those tribes became debris on their own lands:
Captain Jack's wide face above the rope,
his Modoc women dead with twitching hands.

The last and the most splendid, Nez Percé
Chief Joseph, fluttering eagles through Idaho,
dashed his pony-killing getaway.

They got him. Repeating rifles bored at his head
and in one fell look Chief Joseph saw the game
out of that spiral mirror all explode.

Back of the Northwest map their country goes,
mountains yielding and hiding, fold on fold,
gorged with yew trees that were good for bows.

WILLIAM STAFFORD

OREGON WINTER

The rain begins. This is no summer rain,
Dropping the blotches of wet on the dusty road:
This rain is slow, without thunder or hurry:
There is plenty of time—there will be months of rain.
  Lost in the hills, the old gray farmhouses
Hump their backs against it, and smoke from their chim-
        neys
Struggles through weighted air. The sky is sodden with
        water,
It sags against the hills, and the wild geese,
Wedge-flying, brush the heaviest cloud with their wings.
  The farmers move unhurried. The wood is in,
The hay has long been in, the barn lofts piled
Up to the high windows, dripping yellow straws.

There will be plenty of time now, time that will smell of
        fires,
And drying leather, and catalogues, and apple cores.
    The farmers clean their boots, and whittle, and drowse.

JEANNE MC GAHEY

from *CALIFORNIA WINTER*

. . . this land grows the oldest living things,
Trees that were young when Pharaohs ruled the world,
Trees whose new leaves are only just unfurled.
Beautiful they are not; they oppress the heart
With gigantism and with immortal wings;
And yet one feels the sumptuousness of this dirt.

KARL SHAPIRO

THE REDWOODS

Mountains are moving, rivers
are hurrying. But we
are still.

We have the thoughts of giants—
clouds, and at night the stars.

And we have names—gutteral, grotesque—
Hamet, Og—names with no syllables.

And perish, one by one, our roots
gnawed by the mice. And fall.

164

And are too slow for death, and change
to stone. Or else too quick,

like candles in a fire. Giants
are lonely. We have waited long

for someone. By our waiting, surely
there must be someone at whose touch

our boughs would bend; and hands
to gather us; a spirit

to whom we are light as the hawthorn tree.
O if there is a poet

let him come now! We stand at the Pacific
like great unmarried girls,

turning in our heads the stars and clouds,
considering whom to please.

LOUIS SIMPSON

Rolling Waters

Down the great Valley, twenty-five hundred miles from Minnesota,
Carrying every rivulet and brook, creek and rill,
Carrying all the rivers that run down two-thirds the continent—
The Mississippi runs to the Gulf.

—PARE LORENTZ

from THE RIVER

Down the Yellowstone, the Milk, the White and Chey-
enne;
The Cannonball, the Musselshell, the James and the
Sioux;
Down the Judith, the Grand, the Osage, and the Platte,
The Skunk, the Salt, the Black, and Minnesota;
Down the Rock, the Illinois, and the Kankakee
The Allegheny, the Monongahela, Kanawha, and Mus-
kingum;
Down the Miami, the Wabash, the Licking and the Green
The Cumberland, the Kentucky, and the Tennessee;
Down the Ouachita, the Wichita, the Red, and Yazoo—
Down the Missouri, three thousand miles from the Rock-
ies;
Down the Ohio, a thousand miles from the Alleghenies;
Down the Arkansas, fifteen hundred miles from the Great
Divide;
Down the Red, a thousand miles from Texas;
Down the great Valley, twenty-five hundred miles from
Minnesota,
Carrying every rivulet and brook, creek and rill,
Carrying all the rivers that run down two-thirds the
continent—
The Mississippi runs to the Gulf.

PARE LORENTZ

AMERICAN CHILD

Lucky the living child, born in a land
Bordered by rivers of enormous flow:
Missouri talking through its throat of sand,
Mississippi growling under snow,
A country confident that day or night,
Planting, ploughing or at evening rest,
It has a trust like childhood, free of fright,
Having such powers to hold it east and west.

Water edged with willow gray or green
Edges the hours and meadows where she plays.
Where the black earth and the bright time are piled
She lives between those rivers as between
Her birth and death, and is in these bold days
A water-watched and river-radiant child.

PAUL ENGLE

THE RIVERS REMEMBER

Tidewater born he was, and ever
Water flowed with his life. Clear streams,—
Loitering creek and headlong river,—
Followed his steps and marked his dreams.

He opened his eyes on the light of day
Where old Potomac, kingly and wide,
Rounded a green bluff toward a bay;
His cradle rocked with its rocking tide.

He played by another that swifter went—
Rappahannock; and wandered down,
Watching the dark sails seaward bent,
Bound for England from Frederick's town.

He forded westward the blue Rivanna,
The Rapidan, on a lifting trail;
The Shenandoah and the Susquehanna
Took his shadow and heard his hail.

He rode by a river. The James was old,
But the rider was young, with an eager rein,
And spring in Virginia flecked with gold,
And love at the turn of a country lane.

He crossed a river as dark as night
Through storm and peril that few would dare,
With courage leading, a quenchless light;
That light still shines on the Delaware.

Weary and gaunt, he stood by a river,
Its water burning with autumn flame,
And pledged his land to freedom forever;
The York runs yet to the sound of his name.

He sleeps by a river. The same broad flow
That rocked his cradle now guards his rest,
Solemnly moving, as long ago,
The proud wide water he loved the best.

Tidewater born and tidewater bred . . .
The rivers remember. On and on,
Outward, oceanward, worldward led,
They bear the glory of Washington!

NANCY BYRD TURNER

THE RIVER BOATS

Where are the old side-wheelers now,
The river boats of yesteryear—
The *Comet* and *Vesuvius*
Whose whistles sharp and clear
Routed a parish from its bed,
Shaking the morning air?

(Sing low, O voices from the past—
Breathe deep, O honeysuckle flower!)

Where is the shining *Prince of Wales,*
The *Washington* and *Southern Belle,*
The *Sea Gull* and the *Unicorn*
That made the Mississippi swell
In bright, swift tides against the wharves?
Where are they now? Who can tell?

(Play soft, O banjo from the shadows,
Bleed red, O melon on the vine!)

Where does the *Annie Laurie* rest,
The bold *Diana's* fabled hull,
The *Sally Robinson* trail her smoke?

Proud as a lady and beautiful
Casting her shadow in the sun,
Where steams the *Belle Creole?*

(Finger the willows gently, wind,
Spill all your silver, delta moon!)

Where are the boats of yesteryear?
It is a secret I cannot keep:
Deep in the harbor of a dream
They drift with tall majestic sweep,
The song of stevedores long silent,
And all their pilots fast asleep.

DANIEL WHITEHEAD HICKY

WILDERNESS RIVERS

There are rivers
That I know,
Born of ice
And melting snow,
White with rapids,
Swift to roar,
With no farms
Along their shore,
With no cattle
Come to drink
At a staid
And welcoming brink,

With no millwheel
Ever turning
In that cold,
Relentless churning.

Only deer
And bear and mink
At those shallows
Come to drink;
Only paddles
Swift and light
Flick that current
In their flight.
I have felt
My heart beat high,
Watching
With exultant eye
Those pure rivers
Which have known
No will, no purpose
But their own.

ELIZABETH COATSWORTH

WHEN THE DRIVE GOES DOWN
A Lumberjack's Story

There's folks that like the good dry land, an' folks that
    like the sea,
But rock an' river, shoal an' sand, are good enough for
    me.
There's folks that like the ocean crest, an' folks that like
    the town—
But when I really feel the best is when the drive goes
    down.

    So pole away, you river rats,
      From landin' down to lake—
    There's miles of pine to keep in line,
      A hundred jams to break!

There's folks that like to promenade along the boulevard,
But here's a spot I wouldn't trade for all their pavement
    hard;
Ten thousand logs by currents birled an' waters white
    that hiss—
Oh, where's the sidewalk in the world that's half as fine
    as this?

    So leap away, you river rats,
      From landin' down to sluice;
    There's logs to run, there's peavy fun
      To break the timber loose!

DOUGLAS MALLOCH

THE NEGRO SPEAKS OF RIVERS

I've known rivers:
I've known rivers ancient as the world and older than
 the flow of human blood in human veins.

My soul has grown deep like the rivers.

I bathed in the Euphrates when dawns were young.
I built my hut near the Congo and it lulled me to sleep.
I looked upon the Nile and raised the pyramids above it.
I heard the singing of the Mississippi when Abe Lincoln
 went down to New Orleans, and I've seen its
 muddy bosom turn all golden in the sunset.

I've known rivers:
Ancient, dusky rivers.

My soul has grown deep like the rivers.

LANGSTON HUGHES

SONG OF THE CHATTAHOOCHEE

Out of the hills of Habersham,
 Down the valleys of Hall,
I hurry amain to reach the plain,
Run the rapid and leap the fall,
Split at the rock and together again,
Accept my bed, or narrow or wide,

And flee from folly on every side
With a lover's pain to attain the plain
   Far from the hills of Habersham,
   Far from the valleys of Hall.

   All down the hills of Habersham,
   All through the valleys of Hall,
The rushes cried *Abide, abide,*
The willful waterweeds held me thrall,
The laving laurel turned my tide,
The ferns and the fondling grass said *Stay,*
The dewberry dipped for to work delay,
And the little reeds sighed *Abide, abide,*
   Here in the hills of Habersham,
   Here in the valleys of Hall.

   High o'er the hills of Habersham,
   Veiling the valleys of Hall,
The hickory told me manifold
Fair tales of shade, the poplar tall
Wrought me her shadowy self to hold,
The chestnut, the oak, the walnut, the pine,
Overleaning, with flickering meaning and sign,
Said, *Pass not, so cold, these manifold*
   Deep shades of the hills of Habersham,
   These glades in the valleys of Hall.

   And oft in the hills of Habersham,
   And oft in the valleys of Hall,
The white quartz shone, and the smooth brook-stone
Did bar me of passage with friendly brawl,
And many a luminous jewel lone
—Crystals clear or a-cloud with mist,
Ruby, garnet and amethyst—

Made lures with the lights of streaming stone
  In the clefts of the hills of Habersham,
  In the beds of the valleys of Hall.

But oh, not the hills of Habersham,
  And oh, not the valleys of Hall
Avail: I am fain for to water the plain.
Downward the voices of Duty call—
Downward, to toil and be mixed with the main.
The dry fields burn, and the mills are to turn,
And a myriad flowers mortally yearn,
And the lordly main from beyond the plain
  Calls o'er the hills of Habersham,
  Calls through the valleys of Hall.

SIDNEY LANIER

BY SANDY WATERS

Much have I roved by Sandy River
Among the spring-bloomed thyme,
Where love and life go on forever
And where I've spun my rhyme.

Much have I loved by Sandy River
Girls with the light brown hair;
I thought love would go on forever,
Spring be forever fair.

The Spring for mountains goes forever
But not for us who fade
In love and life by Sandy River
Before our dreams are made—

Before our dust goes back forever
To mountain earth we've known;
Before the sweet thyme blossoms hither
Among the gray sand-stone.

I pray the music from this river
Will sing for them and me;
Will sing for us, for us forever,
In our eternity.

JESSE STUART

EAST RIVER
(New York)

The crazy tugs
In the crazy harbor
Wear overalls
And suspenders,
The uniform
Of the working river.

Greased by sun,
Glazed by air,
They nuzzle the flank
Of the ocean liner,
Explode with laughter
At its departure.

Now serve the rich,
Now know the poor,
They sloth at last
In the quiet harbor,
Sloth and sleep
For final pasture.

Against the green moss
Of the pier
They list like buddies
At a bar,
Stagger for stagger,
Star for star.

ROSEMARY THOMAS

DOWN THE MISSISSIPPI
Embarkation

Dull masses of dense green,
The forests range their sombre platforms;
Between them silently, like a spirit,
The river finds its own mysterious path.

Loosely the river sways out, backward, forward,
Always fretting the outer side;
Shunning the invisible focus of each crescent,
Seeking to spread into shining loops over fields.

Like an enormous serpent, dilating, uncoiling,
Displaying a broad scaly back of earth-smeared gold;
Swaying out sinuously between the dull motionless forests,
As molten metal might glide down the lip of a vase of
    dark bronze;

It goes, while the steamboat drifting out upon it,
Seems now to be floating not only outwards but upwards;
In the flight of a petal detached and gradually moving
    skyward
Above the pink explosion of the calyx of the dawn.

JOHN GOULD FLETCHER

THE MOUTH OF THE HUDSON

A single man stands like a bird-watcher,
and scuffles the pepper and salt snow
from a discarded, gray
Westinghouse Electric cable drum.
He cannot discover America by counting
the chains of condemned freight-trains
from thirty states. They jolt and jar
and junk in the siding below him.
He has trouble with his balance.
His eyes drop,
and he drifts with the wild ice
ticking seaward down the Hudson,
like the blank-sides of a jig-saw puzzle.

The ice ticks seaward like a clock.
A Negro toasts
wheat-seeds over the coke-fumes
in a punctured barrel.
Chemical air
sweeps in from New Jersey,
and smells of coffee.

Across the river,
ledges of suburban factories tan
in the sulphur-yellow sun
of the unforgivable landscape.

ROBERT LOWELL

from THE RIVER

Black spruce and Norway pine,
Douglas fir and Red cedar,
Scarlet oak and Shagbark hickory.
We built a hundred cities and a thousand towns—
But at what a cost!
We cut the top off the Alleghenies and sent it down the
        river.
We cut the top off Minnesota and sent it down the river.
We cut the top off Wisconsin and sent it down the river.
We left the mountains and the hills slashed and burned,
And moved on.
We built a hundred cities and a thousand towns—
But at what a cost!
Poor land makes poor people.
Poor people make poor land.

We got the blacks to plant the cotton and they gouged
the top off the valley.
We got the Swedes to cut the forests, and they sent them
down the river.
Then we left a hollow-eyed generation to peck at the
worn-out valley;
And left the Swedes to shiver in their naked North
country.
1903, 1907, 1913, 1922, 1927, 1936, 1937—
For you can't wall out and dam two-thirds the water in
the country.
We built dams but the dams filled in.
We built a thousand-mile dyke but it didn't hold;
So we built it higher.
We played with a continent for fifty years.

Flood control? Of the Mississippi?
Control from Denver to Helena;
From Itasca to Paducah;
From Pittsburgh to Cairo—
Control of the wheat, the corn and the cotton land;
Control enough to put back a thousand forests;
Control enough to put the river together again before it
is too late . . . before it has picked up the heart of
a continent and shoved it into the Gulf of Mexico.

PARE LORENTZ

BY A LAKE IN MINNESOTA

Upshore from the cloud—
The slow whale of country twilight—
The spume of light falls into valleys
Full of roses.

And below,
Out of the placid waters,
Two beavers, mother and child,
Wave out long ripples
To the dust of dead leaves
On the shore.

And the moon walks,
Hunting for hidden dolphins
Behind the darkening combers
Of the ground.

And downshore from the cloud,
I stand, waiting
For dark.

JAMES WRIGHT

AUTUMN SQUALL—LAKE ERIE

The wind has blown that searchlight out
  That people call the moon,
And piled the beach of heaven high
  With dune on cloudy dune.

He's whipped the water till the waves
  Have bared their angry teeth;
They try to gobble up the shore
  And, failing, hiss and seethe.

Old Erie has his dander up
  And heaves with roiling motion—
These autumn nights I think that he
  Imagines he's the ocean.

LOLA INGRES RUSSO

OKEFENOKEE SWAMP

Here is a world which slowed the hands of time,
Choked back the seasons, the minutes and the hours,
Bound east and west by crocodile and slime,
Northward and south by cypress and scarlet flowers.

185

Here thin moons ripen as a lily will
Shredded by shadows on the blackened glass
Of stagnant rivers; slumbering copperheads coil
Where spiders break green backbones of the grass.

There is a music here lost long to man,
Silence beyond a mortal's heart to know;
Flash of swift wings afire, the secret span
Of feathers drifting white as drifts of snow.

Yet always fear, fear burning when quiets cease
Over the hyacinths breathing with guarded breath,
This wild world knowing, as other worlds, that peace
Trembles red-eyed before the claws of death.

DANIEL WHITEHEAD HICKY

IN THE BAYOU

Lazy and slow, through the snags and trees
   Move the sluggish currents, half asleep;
Around and between the cypress knees,
   Like black, slow snakes the dark tides creep—
How deep is the bayou beneath the trees?
"Knee-deep,
    Knee-deep,
      Knee-deep,
        Knee-deep!"
Croaks the big bullfrog of Reelfoot Lake
From his hiding-place in the draggled brake.

What is the secret the slim reeds know
That makes them to shake and to shiver so,
And the scared flags quiver from plume to foot?—
The frogs pipe solemnly, deep and slow:
"Look under
    the root!
      Look under
        the root!"
The hoarse frog croaks and the stark owl hoots
Of a mystery moored in the cypress roots.

Was it love turned hate? Was it friend turned foe?
Only the frogs and the gray owl know,
   For the white moon shrouded her face in a mist
At the spurt of a pistol, red and bright—
At the sound of a shriek that stabbed the night—
   And the little reeds were frightened and whist;
But always the eddies whimper and choke,
And the frogs would tell if they could, for they croak:

> "Deep, deep!
>   Death-deep!
>   Deep, deep!
>   Death-deep!"
> And the dark tide slides and glisters and glides
> Snakelike over the secret it hides.

DON MARQUIS

BIG DAM

Muddy meek river, oh, it was splendid sport
Those times you tore apart tranquility
And swam the gar through frightened village streets
(And sent the villagers to live in tents)
And spread your silted bed on every sort
Of floor, and rammed the prairie at the sea—
But where, do you think, is the end of suchlike feats?
Good Lord, did you never hear of consequence?

Look, do you see your wedge of tumult spread?
Words rage like water, and all Congress frowns,
And tit for tat, and the world witnesses
You shall be damned and dammed for tumult's sake—
And swim the carp above the milking shed
(And send the farmers off to live in towns)
And try if cedars can be cypresses
And lose the arid prairie in a lake.

W. R. MOSES

*   *   *   *   *

SHENANDOAH

Oh, Shenandoah, I long to hear you,
  Away, you rolling river,
Oh, Shenandoah, I long to hear you,
  Away, we're bound away,
  'Cross the wide Missouri.

The white man loved the Indian maiden,
  Away, you rolling river,
With notions his canoe was laden,
  Away, we're bound away,
  'Cross the wide Missouri.

Oh, Shenandoah, I love your daughter,
  Away, you rolling river,
I'll take her 'cross the rolling water,
  Away, we're bound away,
  'Cross the wide Missouri.

Oh, Shenandoah, I'm bound to leave you,
  Away, you rolling river,
Oh, Shenandoah, I'll not deceive you,
  Away, we're bound away,
  'Cross the wide Missouri.

AUTHOR UNKNOWN

Sidewalks of America

This is the wondrous city,
    Where worlds and nations meet;
Say not romance is napping;
    Behold the city street!

—MORRIS ABEL BEER

MANHATTAN

There's Asia on the avenue,
  And Europe in the street,
And Africa goes plodding by
  Beneath my window-seat.

This is the wondrous city,
  Where worlds and nations meet;
Say not romance is napping;
  Behold the city street!

MORRIS ABEL BEER

MANHATTAN LULLABY
(*For Richard—one day old*)

Now lighted windows climb the dark,
  The streets are dim with snow.
Like tireless beetles, amber-eyed,
  The creeping taxis go.
Cars roar through caverns made of steel,
  Shrill sounds the siren horn,
And people dance and die and wed—
  And boys like you are born.

RACHEL FIELD

RECUERDO

We were very tired, we were very merry—
We had gone back and forth all night on the ferry.
It was bare and bright, and smelled like a stable—
But we looked into a fire, we leaned across a table,
We lay on the hill-top underneath the moon;
And the whistles kept blowing, and the dawn came soon.

We were very tired, we were very merry—
We had gone back and forth all night on the ferry;
And you ate an apple, and I ate a pear,
From a dozen of each we had bought somewhere;
And the sky went wan, and the wind came cold,
And the sun rose dripping, a bucketful of gold.

We were very tired, we were very merry—
We had gone back and forth all night on the ferry.
We hailed, "Good morrow, mother!" to a shawl-covered
        head,
And bought a morning paper, which neither of us read;
And she wept, "God bless you!" for the apples and the
        pears,
And we gave her all our money but our subway fares.

EDNA ST. VINCENT MILLAY

CENTRAL PARK TOURNEY

Cars
In the Park
With long spear lights
Ride at each other
Like armored knights;
Rush,
Miss the mark,
Pierce the dark,
Dash by!
Another two
Try.

Staged
In the Park
From dusk
To dawn,
The tourney goes on:
Rush,
Miss the mark,
Pierce the dark,
Dash by!
Another two
Try.

MILDRED WESTON

A CONEY ISLAND LIFE

Having lived a Coney Island life
on rollercoaster ups and downs
and seen my helium hopes
break skyward without me,
now arms filled with dolls
I threw so much for
I take perhaps my last ride
on this planet-carousel
and ask
how many more times round
I have
to catch that brass-ring-sun
before the game is up.

JAMES L. WEIL

LEGEND

I wonder where it could of went to;
  I know I seen it just as plain:
A beautiful, big fairy city
  Shinin' through the rain.

Rain it was, not snow—in winter!
  Special-order April weather
Ticklin' at our two faces
  Pressed up close together.

Not a single soul was near us
  Standin' out there on the bow;
When we passed another ferry
  He says, sudden, "Now!"

Then I looked where he was pointin' . . . .
  I seen a magic city rise . . . .
Gleamin' windows, like when fields is
  Full of fire-flies.

Towers an' palaces in the clouds, like,
  Real as real, but nice and blurred.
"Oh!" I starts in—but he whispers
  "Hush! Don't say a word!

"Don't look long, and don't ast questions,
  Elset you make the fairies sore.
They won't let you even see it
  Never any more.

"Don't you try to ever go there—
   It's to dream of, not to find.
Lovely things like that is always
   Mostly in your mind."

Somethin' made me say, "It's Jersey!" . . . .
   Somethin' mean . . . He hollers, "Hell!
Now you done it, sure as shootin',
   Now you bust the spell!"

Sure enough, the towers and castles
   Went like lightnin' out of sight . . . .
Nothin' there but filthy Jersey
   On a drizzly night.

JOHN V. A. WEAVER

BOSTON

And this is good old Boston,
   The home of the bean and the cod,
Where the Lowells talk to the Cabots,
And the Cabots talk only to God.

J. C. BOSSIDY

THE NEW ORDER

And here is dear old Boston,
The home of the family tree,
Where the Cabots converse with the Kennedys
And the Kennedys talk on TV.

PHYLLIS MC GINLEY

RULERS: PHILADELPHIA

It is said that many a king in troubled Europe would sell
his crown for a day of happiness.
I have seen a monarch who held tightly the jewel of happiness.
On Lombard Street in Philadelphia, as evening dropped
to earth, I gazed upon a laborer duskier than a sky
devoid of moon. He was seated on a throne of flour
bags, waving his hand imperiously as two small
boys played on their guitars the ragtime tunes of
the day.
God's blessing on the monarch who rules on Lombard
Street in Philadelphia.

FENTON JOHNSON

PITTSBURGH

Coming upon it unawares,
A town of men and millionaires,
A town of coal-dust and of churches,
I thought of moons, I thought of birches,
Goals forgotten in the faces
Of the swift who run the races,
Whip-poor-wills and misty meadows,
Musk-rats in the river-shadows,
Robins whistling five o'clock,
Mornings naked on a rock.

WITTER BYNNER

VIEW OF THE CAPITOL FROM THE LIBRARY OF CONGRESS

Moving from left to left, the light
is heavy on the Dome, and coarse.
One small lunette turns it aside
and blankly stares off to the side
like a big white old wall-eyed horse.

On the east steps the Air Force Band
in uniforms of Air Force blue
is playing hard and loud, but—queer—
the music doesn't quite come through.

It comes in snatches, dim then keen,
then mute, and yet there is no breeze.
The giant trees stand in between.
I think the trees must intervene,

catching the music in their leaves
like gold-dust, till each big leaf sags.
Unceasingly the little flags
feed their limp stripes into the air,
and the band's efforts vanish there.

Great shades, edge over,
give the music room.
The gathered brasses want to go
boom——boom.

ELIZABETH BISHOP

NEW ORLEANS

I am a trombone. By the chinaberry tree,
Under virgin's bower in the purple air,
I made a dirty noise you could almost see.
Arabesques edged the house with care
And voices crumbled in a distant square.
O King of the Zulus, consecrate me!
Mamselle's gown was a laugh of lace,
Band played "Dixie" at a thumping pace,
Moon sprawled low with a fire in her face,
And I brayed just once, deliciously.
Man said, "Boy, don't you know your place?"
O King of the Zulus, consecrate me!

HAYDEN CARRUTH

A SIDING NEAR CHILLICOTHE

From the high deck of Santa Fe's El Capitan
cabs; sand-domes, stacks were seen above the box-car line:
old locomotives parked, antedeluvian

in cruel progress, gone before us to that night
toward which we see, sacks of memories, slide in blander
    airs,
and streamline our old eyes and thoughts from glass and
    flight.

Our ears, boys' ears, and eyes and hearts were haunted by
huge hoots of laughter down the dark: the glow: the
    steam
bulging in black and red up the spark-shotten sky.

Now wheels, rails rust together, dews and sunshine eat
the iron grace: through silence their corrosion ticks
and drops in red dust, junk of grandeurs obsolete.

So, like old elephants who stumbled off to die
in their known place, and rot their bulks from ivory
    bones,
the locomotives stood against the prairie sky.

RICHMOND LATTIMORE

DETROIT

There is a cool river
which flows among the red and yellow
pennants of the gas stations,
and through the black brick
of the car factories.
Smoke does not dirty it.
Children splash through it
on their Lambrettas.
It does not disturb the drought
which burns the evergreens
on the square lawns of foremen.
Yet willows grow
from the moss on the bank.
Under the mist of the branches
sit William Blake,
Thomas Jefferson,
Huckleberry Finn,
and Henry James.
They are thinking about fish.
They are watching the river: it flows
through the city of America
without fish.

DONALD HALL

TONIGHT IN CHICAGO . . .

It's a sitting-pretty, windy-city kind of a place.
It's a dine-au-Chateau, lake-shore-below,
Kind of a place.
It's the Loop and the Mart, a great city's heart;
It's a quiet-and-gentle, elegantal, Continental
Kind of a place.
A sprawl-in, sit-tall-in kind of a place.

A quiet lair, a want-to-be-there, a welcome face
Kind of a place.
It's a tall-one-all-tinkly, a smile-all-wrinkly.
It's a wonderful food, wonderful mood,
Kind of a place.
It's excitement and fun, adventure begun, a
Candlelight and spotlight
Kind of a place.

AUTHOR UNKNOWN

LA CROSSE AT NINETY MILES
AN HOUR

Better to be the rock above the river,
The bluff, brown and age-old sandstone,
Than the broad river winding to the Gulf.

The river looks like world reality
And has the serenity of wide and open things.
It is a river of even ice today.

Winter men in square cold huts have cut
Round holes to fish through: I saw it as a boy.
They have a will to tamper with the river.

Up on the high bluffs nothing but spirit!
It is there I would be, where an Indian scout was
Long ago, now purely imaginary.

It is a useless and heaven-depended place,
Commodious rock to lock the spirit in,
Where it gazes on the river and the land.

Better to be rock-like than river-like;
Water is a symbol will wear us all away.
Rock comes to the same end, more slowly so.

Rock is the wish of the spirit, heavy symbol,
Something to hold to beyond worldly use.
I feel it in my bones, kinship with vision,

And on the brown bluffs above the Mississippi
In the land of my deepest, earliest memories,
Rushing along at ninety miles an hour,

I feel the old elation of the imagination.
Strong talk of the river and the rock.
Small division between the world and spirit.

RICHARD EBERHART

OLD DUBUQUE

There is no past, present and future time
here in Dubuque, there is just Dubuque time.—Richard Bissell

From Grant's grave Galena
we drove down in a daze
(from two days of antiques)
to the Mississippi,
then crossed over at noon
to old, hunchbacked Dubuque:
a never-say-die town,
a gray, musty pawnshop,
still doing business; while
on the bluff, blue jeans flap
in a river wind laced
with fresh paint and dead carp.

We couldn't find the house
where she once lived and died
(at ninety, baking bread)
somewhere in the hard maze
of crusty shops and streets.

And Dubuque is a spry,
goofy-sad river gal,
lost in a patchwork-haze
of tears and years gone by;
and I love this mad place
like my dead grandmother
loved her steins of Star beer.

DAVE ETTER

SALT LAKE CITY

When the great golden eagle of the West
Circles this capitol's dome, his wingtips
Ring on the mountains' bell
And the fountains of the sky drench us
In gold. Imagine every white stone,
Each citron brick, immaculate as cloisonné.

              The eagle,
Turning outward, perceives the salt desert
And the bleached skeletons reposing there,
But our streets are straight as our hearts
And prosperous as faith. This is the place
We call the great golden city of the West.

Like the rattler upon the mountain, we
Are free, aloof, but when we strike we warn.
We say we have made the dream of the West
Come true, and the centuries

Pivot upon our clean hearts which know
Success in America, death on the western
Trail, starvation singing through marimba
Ribs, the salt desert, and crazy religion.

HAYDEN CARRUTH

HOUSE IN DENVER

I can remember looking cross-lots from
This house over the evening thistle and
The bee flowers, watching people coming home
From downtown. In the morning I could stand
A long time watching my father disappear
Beyond the sunflowers which you noticed farther
In the morning. Now high buildings interfere
In piles of shining masonry, but are there
Walls yet to come no more secure than these?
My city has not worn its shadows long
Enough to quiet even prairie bees.
I often hear a droning sunflower song
Dissolving the steel, and mark a thistle turning
A curling wall back when I'm thistle-burning.

THOMAS HORNSBY FERRIL

CITY: SAN FRANCISCO

In the morning the city
Spreads its wings
Making a song
In stone that sings.

In the evening the city
Goes to bed
Hanging lights
About its head.

LANGSTON HUGHES

TRIP: SAN FRANCISCO

I went to San Francisco.
I saw the bridges high
Spun across the water
Like cobwebs in the sky.

LANGSTON HUGHES

AT CARMEL

There are people go to Carmel
To see the blue bay pass
Through green wave to white foam
Like snow on new grass.
But I go to hear the auklets crying
Like dark glass on glass.

I go to hear the herons talk
The way that herons have, half asleep,
As they come in past Carmel bar
With a slow wing sweep;
To hear the wood teams jingling up from Sur,
And the contented blether of the Mission sheep.

MARY AUSTIN

APARTMENT HOUSE

A filing-cabinet of human lives
Where people swarm like bees in tunneled hives,
Each to his own cell in the towered comb,
Identical and cramped—we call it home.

GERALD RAFTERY

MANHOLE COVERS

The beauty of manhole covers—what of that?
Like medals struck by a great savage khan,
Like Mayan calendar stones, unliftable, indecipherable,
Not like old electrum, chased and scored,
Mottoed and sculptured to a turn,
 But notched and whelked and pocked and smashed
With the great company names:
Gentle Bethlehem, smiling United States.
This rustproof artifact of my street,
Long after roads are melted away, will lie
Sidewise in the grave of the iron-old world,
Bitten at the edges,
Strong with its cryptic American,
Its dated beauty.

KARL SHAPIRO

CITY AFTERNOON

Far, far down
The earth rumbles in sleep;
Up through its iron grille,
The subway, black as a chimney-
Sweep, growls. An escalator rides
On dinosaur spines
Toward day. And on beyond,
Old bones, bottles,
A dismantled piano, sets
Of Mrs. Humphrey Ward all whirl

In the new disposal unit; above
Its din, apartments are tenanted
Tight as hen-houses, people roosting
In every cupboard. Eighty storeys
Up, pigeons nest on the noise
Or strut above it; higher,
The outcast sun serves its lean meat
Of light.

The whinnying
Of Venetian blinds has ceased: we sit
Invisible in this room,
Behind glass. In a lull,
A chance abatement of sound, a scalping
Silence, far
Down we hear the Iron
Maiden whisper,
Closing upon her spikes.

BARBARA HOWES

SONG OF THE BUILDERS

O beams of steel are slim and black
And danger lurks on the skyward track,
But men are many, and men are bold,
And what is risk, when the stake is gold?
    So riveters ring,
    And hot bolts fly,
    And strong men toil,
    And sweat . . . and die . . .
But the city's towers grow straight and high!

O beams of steel are black and slim,
But the wills of men are stubborn and grim,
They reach forever to clutch the sun,
And what is life, if the goal be won?
        So riveters ring,
        And hot bolts fly,
        And strong men toil,
        And sweat . . . and die . . .
But the city's towers grow straight and high!

JESSIE WILMORE MURTON

SUNDAY

This is the day when all through the town
the cats are keeping store,
the clerks are gone from counter and desk,
the key has turned in the door.

But the cats move about with an owner's airs
over the oranges, apples, and pears,

or among the tins in their rows on the shelves,
proud as merchants and nimble as elves.

Then at last they each lie down to rest
where the big show window is sunniest,

or turn to stare at the passer-by
with a calculating but sleepy eye.

In every one of the fifty states,
in a thousand cities or more,
from Saturday night to Monday at seven
the cats are keeping store!

ELIZABETH COATSWORTH

GEORGIA TOWNS

Deep in the Georgia night when all
The crickets have hushed their notes
And silence lies upon the needles
Of pines and on the feathered throats
Of sparrows in the star-still boughs,
Across the meadows of my mind
There drift the names of Georgia towns
Softly and slowly as summer wind.

O little half-hid towns I love!
I hear them waking, and in sleep,
And all the music of their names
Like opening flowers, a tidal sweep,
Rests on my heart the hand of peace.
O little towns how close you lie
Upon the warm red clay, how near
Your sun-drenched rooftops touch the sky!
Not all the violins in the world,
The flutes, nor ivory keys,
Could take me so triumphantly
And give my soul release.

O Dewy Rose and Talking Rock,
O rain-wet Rising Fawn,
Social Circle where the hand
Of friendship greets the dawn,
O Cave Spring cool as lilies are,
Ty Ty, Ringgold, Summerville
Where honeysuckle haunts the air
When dusk falls blue and chill—
O Blue Ridge resting like a cloud,
Benevolence and Kennesaw,
Hiwassee, Lovelace, Darien
Where four-o'clocks are law,
O Daisytown and Shadydale,
Across my heart you go
With all a June day's fiery breath,
The grace of winter's snow.

Deep in my last dark Georgia night
When I have come to rest,
Am one again with her red clay hills,
May all the names I love the best
Drift back, in music, over me,
May each come ringing like a rhyme
For one who loves each door, each lane,
An old man lost in sleep and Time.

DANIEL WHITEHEAD HICKY

SUMMER CONCERT

We could get the whole town out on a Tuesday night,
With katydids in the trees and bikes in the gutters,
Could get the whole town out, and horns would tootle,
And kids would surge in the grass, and the maestro
    wiggle,
And we'd all twitter like sparrows in creaky hangars,
As culture rustled the aspen back of the high school.

But when we woke to the sizzle the next a.m.,
It was dead, dead, dead under the shingles,
And Sousa was gone, and Bach, and the Army and Navy,
And all we could do to be doing would be to be Wednes-
    day.

REED WHITTEMORE

RURAL DUMPHEAP

This rusty mound of cans,
This scatter of tires and pans,
This litter of mattresses and twisted springs,
This rotting refuse, these abandoned things
Malodorously flung,—this impudent pile
That dares to choke the current, to defile
The innocent season,—all are man's.

Man's inhumanity to sod
Makes countless snowdrops mourn,
And every gentle seed that's born
Gives battle for a dishonored god.

216

Within the heap and darkly, heaves
The growing mutiny of leaves,
While down the valley bird to bird
Relays the rallying word,
And courage calls on every breeze
To armies of anemones,
And triumph scales the parapet,
A host of violet.

O man, where is thy victory?
Despite the blight of tins,
The fern persists and cleaves and wins,
And, gladly, spring begins.

MELVILLE CANE

IN A DESERT TOWN

We have a mountain at the end of our street,
    Changing from day to day;
Sometimes it is prim and distant and neat,
    Vestured in sober gray.

Sunset bewitches it to drift and glow
    Like a castle with opal walls;
Winter transfigures its cliffs with snow
    Into spell-bound waterfalls.

We have a mountain at the end of our street
    Where other towns have a church,
Promising refuge from the clamor and heat
    Like the goal of a weary search.

Moonlight is magical on the mountain, too;
  The shadows grow deep and dim
Till the gazer strays into the dreamy blue
  And sleep comes beckoning him.

Certain that beauty is lingering to greet
  Our homecoming from any place,
Having a mountain at the end of our street
  We do not lack for grace.

LIONEL STEVENSON

COURTHOUSE SQUARE

Uptown there's not a lot of living matter
Left beside the busy people there.
Of course, the pigeons raise a kind of clatter
And clap blue wings together in the air,
And there's a patch of sorry grass between
The cast-iron soldier and the stone marine,
With, now and then, a horse to stand hipshot
Beside a parking meter's grinning slot.

But, by and large, it's gasoline and steel
That give a roar and sputter to uptown.
The hoof has yielded to the racing wheel,
A thousand tailpipes bellow up and down,
And it's small wonder that a staring pig,
Transported through this iron whirligig,
Squeals from his truck in terror and dismay.
He's not the only one to feel that way.

HERBERT MERRILL

MIDWEST TOWN

Farther east it wouldn't be on the map—
  Too small—but here it rates a dot and name.
In Europe it would wear a castle cap
  Or have a cathedral rising like a flame.

But here it stands where the section roadways meet,
  Its houses dignified with trees and lawn;
The stores hold tête-à-tête across Main Street;
  The red brick school, a church—the town is gone.

America is not all traffic lights
  And beehive homes and shops and factories;
No, there are wide green days and starry nights,
  And a great pulse beating strong in towns like these.

RUTH DELONG PETERSON

SATURDAY IN THE COUNTY SEAT

Men halt in the littered spot before the bank
Or on dusty corners—meet each other and stop
To light their blackened pipes, to gossip. Lank,
Sun-wearied sages with sagging trousers prop
Their feet on the parked cars' bumpers to talk, guffaw,
And lament the state of religion, politics, law.
The street is noisy. Women and children crowd
And straggle and dodge through traffic. The pained ear
      rings
With horns and whistles, with voices talking loud
Of sickness and death or crops and the cost of things.
The town wears a veil of dust and smoke above it;
Down here it is raucous and gritty and crude. I love it.

ELIJAH L. JACOBS

CITIES AND SCIENCE

Cities and science serve each other well.
Some cities science built, some not.
Boston was made of bricks and four per cent,
The law, good teaching, medicine, the best museums;
Richmond of pride and culture and good living.
New York is science to the soaring height
Of towers and plumes reflecting down the world;
Compact of steel and tube and cable, rich
In all devices for unloading loads, but poor
In basement bargains on the hundredth floor.
The science-city can be ravishing, as instance
That lace of bridges round the hand-me-up
Of lovable San Francisco. Cities
Are broad and wide and braced
By science in prairie country—Fargo,
Omaha, Topeka; Chicago on the lake,
Milwaukee on the bluff.

DAVID MC CORD

*Americans
Are Always Moving On*

A mericans are always moving on.
It's an old Spanish custom gone astray,
A sort of English fever, I believe,
Or just a mere desire to take French leave,
I couldn't say.

—STEPHEN VINCENT BENÉT

from WESTERN STAR

Americans are always moving on.
It's an old Spanish custom gone astray,
A sort of English fever, I believe,
Or just a mere desire to take French leave,
I couldn't say. I couldn't really say.
But, when the whistle blows, they go away.
Sometimes there never was a whistle blown,
But they don't care, for they can blow their own
Whistles of willow-stick and rabbit-bone,
Quail-calling through the rain
A dozen tunes but only one refrain,
"We don't know where we're going, but we're on our
       way!"

*   *   *   *   *

Oh, paint your wagons with "Pike's Peak or Bust!"
Pack up the fiddle, rosin up the bow,
Vamoose, skedaddle, mosey, hit the grit!
(We pick our words, like nuggets, for the shine,
And, where they didn't fit, we make them fit,
Whittling a language out of birch and pine.)
We're off for Californ-iay,
We're off down the wild O-hi-o!
And every girl on Natchez bluff
Will cry as we go by-o!

*   *   *   *   *

Out of your fever and your moving on,
(Americans, Americans, Americans)
Out of your unassuaged and restless hearts,
Out of your conquest, out of your despair,
I make my song.

STEPHEN VINCENT BENÉT

TRAIL BREAKERS

I

We remember, we do not forget, O Trail Breakers.
Mountain Men, Missourians, following the rivers,
Platte, Yellowstone, Sweetwater, Columbia;
Crossing the Great Divide, the mountain passes,
The dusty cavalcades are coming over the mountains—
The Big Horns, the Wind, the Tetons, the Medicine Bow,
The Bitterroot, the Sierras, the Cascades,
The wind in the Great South Pass remembers the lost
   trappers.

II

Under the red bluffs plod the slow wagon trains, the
   white-tops,
Come the dusty processions along the Oregon Trail and
   the Santa Fe, the lumbering prairie schooners,
Bringing the prairie breakers, the plowmen, the pioneer
   women, bringing the bull-tongue plows
To break the tough sod, in the Dakotas, Nebraska,
Ioway, Minnesota, sowing the corn, the wheat, the golden
   seas.
The pioneer mothers in the sod huts, to breed strong sons
And tall daughters in the sod huts of the Kansas prairie.
To make statebuilders of the West, Montana, Wyoming,
   Washington,
To frame the western democracies, Utah, Colorado, Idaho,
   Nevada, Oregon.

III

Pack train, stage coach, pony express, climb over the
    mountain passes;
The Iron Horse roars west, spouting smoke and cinders,
The continental express streaks on, faster, faster, faster.
On the six-lane highways the sleek speedsters are stream-
    ing west;
The airliner drones across the sky, six hours from coast to
    coast.
The jet plane, the supersonic rocket, trail a white line
    across the blue.
The mushroom blast of the H bomb announces
The terror and the splendor of the
Atomic Age.

JAMES DAUGHERTY

THE PONY EXPRESS

Now into the saddle, and over the grass,
    The galloping race is beginning,
And wild creatures scatter as flying hoofs pass
    Nor guess at the prize in the winning,
As over the prairie from station to station
Rides news on a schedule—and civilization.

Then back past the mountains and over the plains,
    Each messenger prompt to his hour,
They ride through the sun and the snow and the rains
    With words that mean laughter, or power;
And many the watchers in joy or distress
Impatient in hope of the Pony Express!

Today over rails where the streamliners keep
  A schedule exact to the second,
Or into the winds where the silver wings sweep
  Through darkness to landing as reckoned—
How far we have come from the mail's pioneer,
When swift-thudding hoofs won the long race with fear!

DOROTHY BROWN THOMPSON

THE RAILROAD CARS ARE COMING

The great Pacific railway,
  For California hail!
Bring on the locomotive,
  Lay down the iron rail;
Across the rolling prairies
  By steam we're bound to go,
The railroad cars are coming, humming
  Through New Mexico,
The railroad cars are coming, humming
  Through New Mexico.

The little dogs in dog-town
  Will wag each little tail;
They'll think that something's coming
  A-riding on a rail.

The rattlesnake will show its fangs,
    The owl tu-whit, tu-who,
The railroad cars are coming, humming
    Through New Mexico,
The railroad cars are coming, humming
    Through New Mexico.

AUTHOR UNKNOWN

CROSSING

STOP   LOOK   LISTEN
as gate stripes swing down,
count the cars hauling distance
upgrade through town:
warning whistle, bellclang,
engine eating steam,
engineer waving,
a fast-freight dream:
B&M boxcar,
boxcar again,
Frisco gondola,
eight-nine-ten,
Erie and Wabash,
Seaboard, U.P.,
Pennsy tankcar,
twenty-two, three,
Phoebe Snow, B&O,
thirty-four, five,
Santa Fe cattle
shipped alive,
red cars, yellow cars,

orange cars, black,
Youngstown steel
down to Mobile
on Rock Island track,
fifty-nine, sixty,
hoppers of coke,
Anaconda copper,
hotbox smoke,
eighty-eight,
red-ball freight,
Rio Grande,
Nickel Plate,
Hiawatha,
Lackawanna,
rolling fast
and loose,
ninety-seven,
coal car,
boxcar,
CABOOSE!

PHILIP BOOTH

NIGHT JOURNEY

Now as the train bears west,
Its rhythm rocks the earth,
And from my Pullman berth
I stare into the night
While others take their rest.
Bridges of iron lace,
A suddenness of trees,
A lap of mountain mist
All cross my line of sight,
Then a bleak wasted place,
And a lake below my knees.
Full on my neck I feel
The straining at a curve;
My muscles move with steel,
I wake in every nerve.
I watch a beacon swing
From dark to blazing bright;
We thunder through ravines
And gullies washed with light.
Beyond the mountain pass
Mist deepens on the pane;
We rush into a rain
That rattles double glass.
Wheels shake the roadbed stone,
The pistons jerk and shove,
I stay up half the night
To see the land I love.

THEODORE ROETHKE

£ANDSCAPE AS METAL AND FLOWERS

All over America railroads ride through roses.

I should explain this is thoroughly a matter of fact.
Wherever sandy earth is piled to make a road for train
    tracks
The banks on either side are covered with wild, sweet
Pink rambler roses: not because roses are pretty
But because ramblers grow in cheap soil and will hold
The banks firm against rain—therefore the railroad roses.

All over America the steel-supporting flowers,
Sometimes at village depots covering the shingled station,
Sometimes embracing watertanks, but mostly endless ten-
    drils
Out of which locomotives and pullmans flash the morn-
    ing—
And tunnels the other way into whose firm, sweet evening
The whistle fades, dragging freight cars, day coaches and
    the caboose.

WINFIELD TOWNLEY SCOTT

CONTINENTAL CROSSING

"Set back your watches—this is Mountain Time."
We turned the hands, and moved Now back to Then,
Given a second chance to live again
This last hour, differently—as if the dime
Slid through the slot and back, with all it bought.
An unearned hour—and how should it be spent?
In merriment, in dreams of long content,
In private prayer, in philosophic thought,
Pondering time and space to understand?
We cut the deck, and dealt another hand.

DOROTHY BROWN THOMPSON

PROGRESS

There are two ways now
To cross the mountain.

One is a foot-path;
My father walked it beside his *burro,*
The *burro* loaded with eggs in boxes
To trade for *chile* and plums and apples
In Chimayó.

One is a highway;
Your automobile, I watch it climbing
In such a hurry, on easy curvings
That slide beneath you and wave behind you—
Pronto! You pass!

233

The path takes longer;
A week in going, a week in coming;
A man can see more, hear more, and feel more,
Learn more of wisdom in long, slow thinking
    Along the trail.

But, as *señor* says,
We have the highway. All the old wisdom
Does not much matter. If I could buy me
An automobile, I would not trade it
    For any *burro!*

EDITH AGNEW

YOU ARE ON U.S. 40 HEADED WEST
(*Legend on highway markers across Nevada*)

This is Nevada, near the end of one
More day of driving on the slate blue road.
The miles string-stretch into the glare of sun,
The vibrant air presses a weary load
Against your eyes. Your lips and skin are tense
And dry from heat. The wire-looped design
Of telephone poles, like a rambling fence,
Guards you along the highway's lonely line.
Your spattered windshield pushes rays that bend
From tilted distances toward which you ride,
And pungent margins of gray sage extend
Their subtle monotones on either side.
Here space is host, and you the labeled guest:
"You are on U.S. 40 Headed West."

VERA WHITE

SONG OF THE TRUCK

This is the song that the truck drivers hear
In the grinding of brake and the shifting of gear,
From the noise of the wheel and the clarion horn,
From the freight and the weight—
                    a song has been born:
Mohair and cotton and textiles and silk,
Chickens and onions and apples and milk,
Rubber and clothing and coffee and tires,
Harness and hay and molasses and wires,
Petroleum, vinegar, furniture, eggs,
Race horses, stoves, and containers and kegs,
Chemicals, cantaloupes, canned goods and seeds—
Song of the cargo America needs!
Song of the wheels in the well-traveled grooves—
Coastline to coastline—
                    America moves!

DORIS FRANKEL

AMBITION

I got pocketed behind 7X-3824;
He was making 65, but I can do a little more.
I crowded him on the curves, but I couldn't get past,
And on the straightaways there was always some truck
        coming fast.
Then we got to the top of a mile-long incline
And I edged her out to the left, a little over the white line,
And ahead was a long grade with construction at the
        bottom,

And I said to the wife, "Now by golly I got 'm!"
I bet I did 85 going down the long grade,
And I braked her down hard in front of the barricade,
And I swung in ahead of him and landed fine
Behind 9W-7679.

MORRIS BISHOP

SOUTHBOUND ON THE FREEWAY

A tourist came in from Orbitville,
parked in the air, and said:

The creatures of this star
are made of metal and glass.

Through the transparent parts
you can see their guts.

Their feet are round and roll
on diagrams or long

measuring tapes, dark
with white lines.

They have four eyes.
The two in back are red.

Sometimes you can see a five-eyed
one, with a red eye turning

on the top of his head.
He must be special—

the others respect him
and go slow

when he passes, winding
among them from behind.

They all hiss as they glide,
like inches, down the marked

tapes. Those soft shapes,
shadowy inside

the hard bodies—are they
their guts or their brains?

MAY SWENSON

UP SILVER STAIRSTEPS

Up silver stairsteps of the wind we rise,
Our great ship leaves the earth's substantial floor;
We climb up in the spacious moonlit skies
Behind four trusted engines' mighty roar . . .
Higher we climb until the lights below
Are golden eggs down in a velvet nest
And motor cars are bugs with lights aglow
On arteries north, south and east and west . . .
What do these matter when we zoom through space
Where clouds sleep on bright mountains of the wind,

When the full moon climbs through clouds and tries to
      race
And our ship cannot leave the moon behind?
Reach out and throw a rock to slow the moon,
Reach out and grab myself a falling star . . .
From Knoxville to Chicago is too soon,
To coast from Heaven down where the world things are.

JESSE STUART

POST EARLY FOR SPACE

Once we were wayfarers, then seafarers, then airfarers;
We shall be spacefarers soon,
Not voyaging from city to city or from coast to coast,
But from planet to planet and from moon to moon.

This is no fanciful flight of imagination,
No strange, incredible, utterly different thing;
It will come by obstinate thought and calculation
And the old resolve to spread an expanding wing.

We shall see homes established on distant planets,
Friends departing to take up a post on Mars;
They will have perils to meet, but they will meet them,
As the early settlers did on American shores.

We shall buy tickets later, as now we buy them
For a foreign vacation, reserve our seat or berth,
Then spending a holiday month on a moon of Saturn,
Look tenderly back to our little shining Earth.

And those who decide they will not make the journey
Will remember a son up there or a favorite niece,
Eagerly awaiting news from the old home-planet,
And will scribble a line to catch the post for space.

PETER J. HENNIKER-HEATON

We Have Tomorrow

We have tomorrow
Bright before us
Like a flame.

—LANGSTON HUGHES

YOUTH

We have tomorrow
Bright before us
Like a flame.

Yesterday
A night-gone thing,
A sun-down name.

And dawn-today
Broad arch above
The road we came.

We march!

LANGSTON HUGHES

LAND OF THE FREE

We don't know

We aren't sure . . .

We wonder whether the dream of American liberty
Was two hundred years of pine and hardwood
And three generations of the grass

And the generations are up: the years over

We don't know

It was two hundred years from the smell of the tidewater
Up through the Piedmont: on through the piney woods:
Till we came out
With our led calves and our lean women
In the oak openings of Illinois

It was three generations from the oak trees—
From the islands of elm and the islands of oak in the
        prairie—
Till we heeled out with our plows and our steel harrows
On the grass-drowned reef bones of the Plains

"Four score and seven years" said the Orator

We remember it differently: we remember it
Kansas: Illinois: Ohio: Connecticut.
We remember it Council Bluffs: St. Louis:
Wills Creek: the Cumberland: Shenandoah

The long harangues of the grass in the wind are our
        histories

We tell our freedom backward by the land

We tell our past by the gravestones and the apple trees

We wonder whether the great American dream
Was the singing of locusts out of the grass to the west
        and the
West is behind us now:

The west wind's away from us

We wonder if the liberty is done:
The dreaming is finished

We can't say

We aren't sure

Or if there's something different men can dream

Or if there's something different men can mean by
        Liberty . . . .

Or if there's liberty a man can mean that's
Men: not land

We wonder

We don't know

We're asking

ARCHIBALD MAC LEISH

from *THE NEW WORLD*

This America is an ancient land,
Conquered and re-conquered by successive races.
It is the Radiant Land and Continent of the Blest
Forever won and forever lost,
And forever seen by that vision which thrilled Balboa
Staring the Pacific;
And forever seen by that revelation of the soul
Which came to John Keats through Homer,
For both seas and land, and visions of a new day may be
      seen,
And gold may be seen by Cortes and Pizarro and their
      sons,
Who turn all Radiant Lands to gold, and starve therefor.
But this New World is forever new to hands that keep it
      new.

*   *   *   *   *

EDGAR LEE MASTERS

THE NEW COLOSSUS

Not like the brazen giant of Greek fame,
With conquering limbs astride from land to land;
Here at our sea-washed sunset gates shall stand
A mighty woman with a torch, whose flame
Is the imprisoned lightning, and her name
Mother of Exiles. From her beacon-hand
Glows world-wide welcome; her mild eyes command
The air-bridged harbor that twin-cities frame.
"Keep, ancient lands, your storied pomp!" cries she
With silent lips. "Give me your tired, your poor,
Your huddled masses yearning to breathe free,
The wretched refuse of your teeming shore.
Send these, the homeless, tempest-tossed to me—
I lift my lamp beside the golden door!"

EMMA LAZARUS

I SING AMERICA NOW!

I shout my words above the blowing wind,
   I sing between the handles of the plow;
My backbone is as hard as stone to bend,
   I am a man: I sing America now!
I sing America's sure destiny:
   The handles of the plow, the dirt, the mules;
Full barns, sheep, cattle, wheat, return of tree,
   Return of men to use the working tools.

This is America if it is to be
   A land of sturdy men with freemen's dreams,
Sturdy as mountains, free as wind is free,
   Plowing the slopes and bottoms by the streams.
Better to chance the grain than chance the gold;
   Better to own your brains than be a slave—
Better to hold a plow, watch soil unfold,
   For time is brief from cradle to the grave.

JESSE STUART

TABLEAU

Locked arm in arm they cross the way,
   The black boy and the white,
The golden splendor of the day,
   The sable pride of night.

From lowered blinds the dark folk stare,
    And here the white folk talk,
Indignant that these two should dare
    In unison to walk.

Oblivious to look and word
    They pass, and see no wonder
That lightning brilliant as a sword
    Should blaze the path of thunder.

COUNTEE CULLEN

REFUGEE IN AMERICA

There are words like *Freedom*
Sweet and wonderful to say.
On my heart-strings freedom sings
All day everyday.

There are words like *Liberty*
That almost make me cry.
If you had known what I knew
You would know why.

LANGSTON HUGHES

from AMERICA WAS PROMISES

America was always promises.
From the first voyage and the first ship there were
    promises—
'the tropic bird which does not sleep at sea'
'the great mass of dark heavy clouds which is a sign'
'the drizzle of rain without wind which is a sure sign'
'the whale which is an indication'
'the stick appearing to be carved with iron'
'the stalk loaded with roseberries'
'and all these signs were from the west'
'and all night heard birds passing.'

America was promises—to whom?

There is Spain Austria Poland China Bohemia.
There are dead men in the pits in all those countries.
Their mouths are silent but they speak. They say
"The promises are theirs who take them."

Listen! Brothers! Generation!
Listen! You have heard these words. Believe it!
Believe the promises are theirs who take them!

Believe unless we take them for ourselves
Others will take them for the use of others!
Believe unless we take them for ourselves
All of us: one here: another there:
Men not Man: people not the People:
Hands: mouths: arms: eyes: not syllables—
Believe unless we take them for ourselves
Others will take them: not for us: for others!

Believe unless we take them for ourselves
Now: soon: by the clock: before tomorrow:
Others will take them: not for now: for longer!

Listen! Brothers! Generation!
Companions of leaves: of the sun: of the slow evenings:
Companions of the many days: of all of them:
Listen! Believe the speaking dead! Believe
The journey is our journey. O believe
The signals were to us: the signs: the birds by
Night: the breaking surf.

ARCHIBALD MAC LEISH

Index of Authors

Index of Titles

255

Index of First Lines

257

ACKNOWLEDGMENTS

Grateful acknowledgment is made to the following authors, publishers, and other copyright holders for permission to reprint copyrighted material: EDITH AGNEW for "Progress" from *Songs of Marcelino* by Edith Agnew, copyright © 1936, 1940, 1953 by Edith Agnew.

APPLETON-CENTURY-CROFTS, affiliate of Meredith Press, for "The Apple-Barrel of Johnny Appleseed" from *Going to the Sun* by Vachel Lindsay, copyright 1923 by D. Appleton and Co.; "The Flower-Fed Buffaloes" from *Going to the Stars* by Vachel Lindsay, copyright 1926 by D. Appleton and Company, copyright renewed 1954 by Elizabeth C. Lindsay; the selection from *The New World* by Edgar Lee Masters, copyright 1937 by D. Appleton & Co.

MORRIS BISHOP for his poem "I Hear America Griping," copyright © 1964 by Morris Bishop.

HARRIET GRAY BLACKWELL for her poem "Hill People," copyright 1953 by Harriet Gray Blackwell, first published in *The Saturday Evening Post*.

ARNA BONTEMPS for his poem "Southern Mansions" from *The Poetry of the Negro, 1746–1949,* an anthology edited by Langston Hughes and Arna Bontemps, published by Doubleday & Co., Inc., 1949.

ARTHUR S. BOURINOT for "A Legend of Paul Bunyan" from *Watcher of Men, Selected Poems, 1947–1966* by Arthur S. Bourinot, copyright 1966 by Arthur S. Bourinot.

BRANDT & BRANDT for "Daniel Boone," "Negro Spirituals," and "Southern Ships and Settlers" from *A Book of Americans* by Rosemary and Stephen Vincent Benét, published by Holt, Rinehart & Winston, Inc., copyright 1933 by Rosemary and Stephen Vincent Benét, copyright renewed © 1961 by Rosemary Carr Benét; "Invocation" and "Robert E. Lee" from *John Brown's Body* by Stephen Vincent Benét, published by Holt, Rinehart & Winston, Inc., copyright 1927, 1928 by Stephen Vincent Benét, copyright renewed © 1955 by Rosemary Carr Benét; the selection from *Western Star* by Stephen Vincent Benét, published by Holt, Rinehart & Winston, Inc., copyright 1943 by Rosemary Carr Benét.

JAMES BROUGHTON for his poem "The Birds of America," first published in *Poetry,* copyright © 1964 by James Broughton.

BRUCE CATTON and AMERICAN HERITAGE PUBLISHING CO., INC., for "Names from the War" from *Names from the War* by Bruce Catton, copyright © 1960 by American Heritage Publishing Co., Inc.

WILLIAM CHILDRESS for "Korea Bound, 1952," reprinted from *Harper's Magazine,* copyright © 1965 by Harper's Magazine, Inc.

THE CHRISTIAN SCIENCE MONITOR for "Post Early for Space" by Peter J. Henniker-Heaton, reprinted from *The Christian Science Monitor,* copyright © 1952 by The Christian Science Publishing Society. All rights reserved.

ELIZABETH COATSWORTH for her poem "Sunday" (originally published in *The New Yorker*), from *Poems* by Elizabeth Coatsworth, copyright © 1957 by The Macmillan Company.

COPYWRITING DEPARTMENT, COLE & WEBER ADVERTISING AGENCY, Seattle, Washington, for their poem "Tonight in Chicago."

COURIER-JOURNAL JOB PRINTING CO., Louisville, Kentucky, for "Kivers" from *Kinfolks: Kentucky Mountain Rhymes* by Ann Cobb, copyright © 1922 by Ann Cobb, published by Houghton Mifflin Company.

COWARD-MCCANN, INC., for "Daniel Webster's Horses" and "The Navajo" from *Compass Rose* by Elizabeth Coatsworth, copyright 1929 by Coward-McCann, Inc.

ABOUT THE COMPILERS

Mrs. Brewton was born in Americus, Georgia, and was graduated from the State Normal School in Athens, Georgia. Dr. Brewton was born in Brewton, Alabama; he was graduated from Howard College in Birmingham, and received his M.A. and Ph.D. from George Peabody College for Teachers in Nashville, Tennessee, where he is now chairman of the English Department. He has also done graduate work at Columbia University.

Dr. and Mrs. Brewton have compiled a number of anthologies of poetry and verse for children, and Dr. Brewton has written many articles on education and children's literature.

The Brewtons are folklore enthusiasts, and they both enjoy gardening in their spare time.

ABOUT THE ILLUSTRATOR

Ann Grifalconi's grandfather was a well-known Lincoln historian, and both she and her mother, author Mary Hays Weik, have an active interest in all facets of American history. It was quite natural, therefore, that Miss Grifalconi was delighted with the prospect of illustrating AMERICA FOREVER NEW.

Miss Grifalconi was born in New York City. She attended Cooper Union, Hunter College, the University of Cincinnati, and received a B.S. degree from New York University. For several years, she taught fine arts in junior and senior high schools in New York City.

After a 15,000-mile auto trip through Europe, Miss Grifalconi wrote a much needed book about camping out on the continent. She has illustrated many books for both children and adults. One of her woodcuts inspired her mother to write *The Jazz Man,* which—with artwork by Miss Grifalconi—was cited by *The New York Times* as one of the ten best-illustrated children's books of the year.